COWBOY-ARTIST

Charles M. Russell

Born: March 19, 1864

Died: October 24, 1926

The biography of the cowboy-artist who preserved the Wild West in paintings and sculpture that will live forever. He painted what he saw with complete realism—gaunt horses, starving cattle, scorched sagebrush. Most marvelously he painted people—mountain men, fur traders, Indians, cowpokes. Riding herd, living among Indians, Charlie Russell drew inspiration from danger, always racing time, for a gaudy era was ending and his life's obsession was to capture it on canvas and record it in bronze.

Books by Shannon Garst

Amelia Earhart: *Heroine of the Skies*
Annie Oakley
Big Foot Wallace of the Texas Rangers
Broken-Hand Fitzpatrick: *Greatest of Mountain Men*
Buffalo Bill
Chief Joseph of the Nez Perces
Cowboy-Artist: *Charles M. Russell*
Custer: *Fighter of the Plains*
Dick Wootton: *Trail Blazer of Raton Pass*
Frontier Hero: *Simon Kenton*
Jack London: *Magnet for Adventure*
James Bowie and His Famous Knife
Joe Meek: *Man of the West*
Kit Carson: *Trail Blazer and Scout*
Scotty Allan: *King of the Dog-Team Drivers*
Sitting Bull: *Champion of His People*
Three Conquistadors: *Cortez, Coronado, Pizarro*
Will Rogers: *Immortal Cowboy*
William Bent and His Adobe Empire

with Warren Garst

Ernest Thompson Seton: *Naturalist*
Wild Bill Hickok

COWBOY-ARTIST

Charles M. Russell

by Shannon Garst

JULIAN MESSNER NEW YORK

Published simultaneously in the United States and Canada by
Julian Messner, a division of Simon & Schuster, Inc.,
1 West 39 Street, New York, N.Y. 10018.

Fourth Printing, 1966

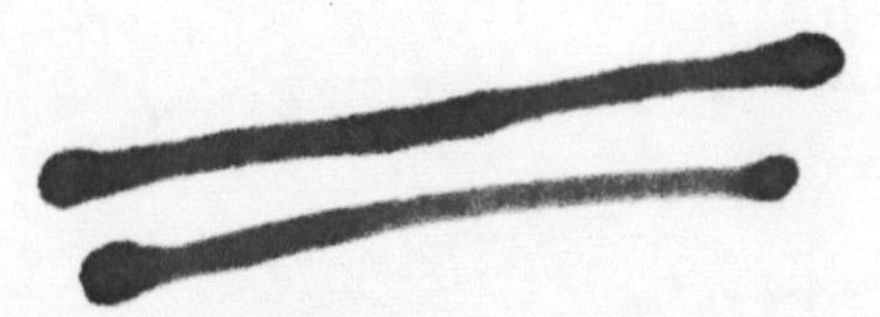

Printed in the United States of America
Library of Congress Catalog Card No. 60-7057

For

Scotty Grey

Acknowledgments

I am grateful to the numerous people who helped me in one way or another in the preparation of this book. My special gratitude goes to Virginia Walton, librarian of the Historical Society of Montana, who, with her efficient staff, made my research a joy. To those many friends of Charles Russell's who added information and highlights on his life or personality, my sincere thanks.

I am grateful for permission to use quotations

From *Good Medicine* by Charles M. Russell.
Copyright 1929, 1930, by Nancy Russell.
Reprinted by permission of Doubleday & Co., Inc.

Also, for permission to quote from the Biographical Note by Nancy C. Russell, from the same volume.

My thanks for the quotation reprinted by permission of the publishers, The Arthur H. Clark Company, from *Granville Stuart's Journals and Reminiscences,* Edited by Paul C. Phillips, page 195, copyrighted 1957.

1

The truant

In the classroom a towheaded boy sat with a large geography book propped in front of him. From the teacher's desk it would have appeared that Charles Russell was intent upon his schoolwork, but such interest was an unnatural state of affairs for this lad. The teacher, however, had his back turned to the room as he worked out an arithmetic problem for the class.

A sudden snicker from the boy across the aisle from Charlie caused Mr. Mack to whirl around, glaring at Charlie, the usual troublemaker. But there was an expression of complete innocence on the Russell boy's face and he appeared to be absorbed in his book. Mr. Mack went back to conducting the arithmetic lesson.

For a time the room was quiet save for the scratching of the chalk on the board and the droning sound of the teacher's voice as he explained the problem.

Then came another snicker, louder and longer this time. Mr. Mack turned around again to stare in the direction of the sound, and this time he caught sight of a boyish grin and a mischievous twinkle in a certain pair of blue eyes. Instantly he strode down the aisle, and Charlie hurriedly thrust something into his desk a moment before Mr. Mack paused beside him.

"Give it to me!" the man demanded.

The boy slowly took the little wax bucking horse he had just finished molding, and reluctantly placed it in the schoolmaster's outstretched hand.

Charlie's elaborate pretense of studying while making the clever little figure had amused his friend across the aisle, who like many schoolboys, was always looking for an excuse to laugh. But Mr. Mack was not amused. His strong fingers closed and opened, and the once-perfect miniature horse was a lump of wax again. The other boy now looked frightened, but it was young Russell who was about to receive the full brunt of Mr. Mack's anger.

Charlie was seized by the back of the collar and dragged to the front of the room where a wooden paddle was briskly applied to the seat of his pants. The boy did not wince or cry, but the moment he was released, instead of facing his classmates in humiliation and returning to his desk as he was told, he darted through the door and was gone.

It was heavenly outside. Spring was in the air. Birds sang as though about to burst their throats with the joy of being alive. Redbud and dogwood were in bloom, turning the countryside around the school into a fragrant, bright wonderland.

Charlie ran until the schoolhouse was out of sight, then he at last slackened his pace and wandered down to the river. The St. Louis waterfront was his favorite spot, for the Mississippi River banks swarmed with the most fascinating assortment of people he had ever seen: mountain men in buckskin, Spaniards wearing colorful costumes, silent-footed Indians wrapped in bright blankets, with feathers in their hair, rough roustabouts, French-Canadian half-breeds with gay-colored sashes. Charlie eyed those broad, gaudy sashes with envy and longing.

From the banks he could watch river craft of all descriptions coming from or sailing to the mysterious land of the West. The incoming boats bore huge bales of buffalo robes and beaver pelts. Adventurers crowded the wharves, their faces wind- and weather-burned, their buckskins dirty and worn. These were the men whose footsteps Charlie dogged, for they had exciting tales to tell of Injun scrapes and other skirmishes in the wilderness.

For the rest of the day he strolled around the supply houses, the wagon yards, the harness and gunsmith shops, watching the activities and eagerly listening to the colorful talk. Whenever he heard such names as Manuel Lisa, Kit Carson, Jim Bridger, Joe Meek, Charlie's heart beat faster. Once in a while someone would mention Bent's Fort and that name really made the boy's heart thump, for William Bent, builder of that fort, was Charlie's greatuncle, as were George Bent, who had been scalped by Comanches, and Charles Bent, who died gallantly during a Mexican insurrection while acting as governor of New Mexico.

The boy knew all about these heroic deeds and was terribly proud of his greatuncles. And after hearing his father read aloud stories of exploration and pioneering, Charlie longed to seek his fame and fortune in the Wild West, as his brave and daring forebears had done.

Further down the wharf he caught sight of men striding up and down the gangplank of a keelboat with a little house built in the middle. They were loading bales and casks, blankets, bolts of bright-colored cloth, all sorts of knickknacks to trade with the Indians for furs.

Charlie heaved a deep sigh as he saw that it was almost ready to shove off. There was a line of ropes from the vessel to men waiting on shore. There was also a herd of horses nearby, evidently to accompany the boat.

Finally everyone was aboard except the boss, who was shouting last-minute directions. Screwing up his nerve, Charlie darted over to the man's side.

"Take me with you!" he said breathlessly. "I'll work hard. Honest I will."

The dark-haired man looked down at him in some surprise, then grinned and put his hand on the tousled fair hair. "The Injuns would sure like this scalp." He chuckled. "They favor straw-colored locks."

But Charlie was not to be scared off. "I can take care of myself," he replied firmly.

"Run on home and wait until you grow up," the man told him. "Even Jim Bridger was older than you when he went West, and he was the youngest lad in the Rockies. He was fifteen. So was Kit Carson."

Charlie's shoulders drooped. "The West'll be nothin' by the time I'm fifteen," he muttered.

"The West will still be wild by the time you're an old man," the trader said over his shoulder as he started up the gangplank. Once on deck, he bellowed: "All set! Sho-o-o-ve off!"

A bell clanged. Men on shore bent shoulders to the ropes; those on the boat used long poles. The horses were urged into motion by two drivers and slowly the keelboat moved out into the sluggish river.

Oh why, Charlie wondered, had he not thought of hiding himself on the boat instead of asking for a job! He could have concealed himself behind some bales until they were far enough up the Mississippi so that he could not be sent back. As he stood there, considering the possibility of stowing away, he glanced up at the sun and suddenly realized that school must be out by now and that he must hurry home so that his latest escapade would not be discovered. He set off at a run and, to shorten the distance, he took a short cut through the woods that stood behind the large white house.

Somewhat out of breath, Charlie dashed into the kitchen where the good smells told him that dinner was almost ready and that there was fresh gingerbread. Suddenly he realized how hungry he was.

"Got any cookies?" he demanded of Mammy Sukey.

"No siree. But there's fresh gingerbread for those who washes their hands and faces and combs their hair and cleans up their plates."

"That won't be hard to do—clean up my plate, I mean. I'm starved."

"You get washed up then."

Charlie carried out this order by dipping his fingertips in water, dabbing them over his mouth, then running his damp fingers through his hair. Even a comb and brush could not subdue his unruly blond hair, so he seldom bothered to try.

Heaving a sigh of relief at being on time, he went into the dining room where the family was already gathering. No embarrassing questions would be asked this time. His brothers were not given to tattling, so he was not especially worried that they would mention the paddling he'd got at school, or his running away afterward.

"Charlie Russell!" his mother said. "How can you get so dirty in a single day? I declare, I never saw your like. And your hair looks as though it hadn't been combed for a week."

The boy hung his head. His mother was an aristocratic-looking, fastidious woman and he adored her although it was beyond him to live up to her ideals of neatness.

His father spoke up: "You ought to be sent from the table, young man. You will be the next time you come to a meal looking so untidy."

Charlie's four brothers looked well pleased with themselves because their appearance did not call for criticism. Baby Sue, the only girl in the family, beamed at her brother from her high-chair, too young to understand or care what was going on. Charlie smiled back at her and was glad when the conversation turned to more pleasant subjects.

That night after supper Charlie worked hard on a letter to the schoolmaster. It stated that he was going to visit an aunt and would not be back at school for some weeks. The next morning he gave the note to Archie, one of his cousins, to deliver. Every day thereafter he climbed into the carriage that took some of the Russell children and some of their numerous cousins to school. Then, when they got to the place where he could best make his way to the river front, he would jump down and hurry to his favorite place.

This went on for about two weeks; then one afternoon as Charlie left from the wharf and was about to start for home, he saw his father coming toward him, his chin whiskers seeming to bristle with anger.

Charlie turned and ran. Darting around a warehouse, he found an open door, slipped inside, and hid behind some large bales of buffalo robes. He remained there with pounding heart until the footsteps died away. It was not fright that made him hide, although he was sure a whipping was in store for him. It was rather his great unwillingness to be sent back to the hated classroom.

He stayed at the waterfront for a week, sleeping in warehouses at night, wandering around watching the activities during the day. Every morning he carefully looked around to see if his angry father was searching for him again, but evidently his family had washed their hands of him. Maybe they didn't want him back . . .

As day followed day, with no one apparently caring where he was, a great feeling of loneliness grew inside him.

He had started out with some money in his pocket—money he had saved up from his allowance—so he had been able to buy food. But now his pocket held only a few coins. He wished that he had all the money he had been saving for the past two years, but his mother had come across it the week before, when she was straightening out his untidy drawers.

"Where did you get all this money?" she had asked him. "There's thirty-seven dollars here!"

"It's from my allowance," he replied frankly. "I've been saving it for when I go West."

"You'll not go West," she had told him emphatically. "At least not until you're a grown man. Your father and I have plans for you, son. You'll go to college; then there'll be a good job waiting for you in your father's company. You don't realize how fortunate you are to have something like that to step into. You won't have to struggle to make a good living the way most young men must do."

Charlie had not been in the least excited at that prospect, and had felt very unhappy when his father took the money and put it in the bank. How he wished he had that money now! If he had it, he would go West and never come back—then maybe his parents would be sorry.

He started looking around the wharf for a job with a trading company or on one of the wagon trains setting out for Santa Fe, but no one seemed eager to take him on.

At last, his money gone, Charlie had to admit that his home was far more comfortable than the dirty old warehouses. As he thought of Mammy Sukey's wonderful cooking, his mouth watered and it seemed to him that he could smell the delicious aroma of freshly baked bread and ginger cookies.

With lagging feet he turned homeward, wondering what would happen to him when he got there. As a rule his father did not believe in whipping his children. Instead, he talked to them in a way that made them want to crawl off into a corner in shame. A few times Charlie had almost wished his father would spank him instead.

When he reached home, however, he found a worse punishment awaiting him. His frail mother was in bed, sick with worry. All his father did was shake his head sadly and say over and over, "Charlie, what are we going to do with you?" His face showed such concern and sorrow that the boy felt more contrite and ashamed than ever.

"I don't want to go back to that horrid old school, Father," Charlie said unhappily.

"You won't be going back." Mr. Russell's voice was stern. "You weren't learning anything there anyway. And from what I hear, you were keeping the others from learning by distracting them with your drawings and wax figures. Next year I'm sending you to the Burlington Military Academy in Burlington, New Jersey."

Charlie's eyes filled with tears despite his effort to hold them back. "But I don't want to go to a military academy. I want to go West."

"If you'll stay at the military academy for a year, and if you still have the notion of going West, I'll send you there as soon as you're sixteen."

Charlie could hardly believe his ears. "Do you mean it?" he cried.

"It's a promise—if you fulfill your part without any more such goings-on as running away and worrying your mother and me into our graves."

"I'm sorry." Charlie almost choked on the words, they were so hard to say, but he was truly repentant.

Summer passed and Charlie, lured by the promised reward, went off to Burlington Military Academy. His short stay there was memorable only for a notebook he left behind filled with sketches of rivermen, Indians, and bucking horses and a record score of demerits that he had to work out by marching guard. He did not mind this punishment as much as he hated being confined indoors with his nose in a book, which is about what studying amounted to with him.

His earliest known painting is a water color done while he was there. Called "A Dream of Burlington," it shows a young man asleep in front of a fireplace. In the distance is a shadowy line of marching cadets; at the top, some boys are engaged in a dormitory pillow fight. But in the center of the picture and dominating it is a wide river with a steamboat embarking.

He still yearned for the waterfront.

He remained at the academy the first term, but when

he came home at vacation time he announced that he would not go back to Burlington.

"But I thought you wanted to go West!" his father said. "My promise to send you there depended on your staying at school a year."

"I still plan to go West someday," Charlie replied.

At their wits' end to know what to do with their son, the Russells finally sent him to an art school, thinking that if he followed his natural bent he would not be so unruly. After attending classes for a week, Charlie came home with his drawing and painting material and announced, "All they would let me do was draw boxes and cones and stuff like that. I want to draw living things. I can draw and paint better than the teacher."

"Your modesty stuns me," his father said sarcastically. "I don't know what to do with you. You must know that you're too young to leave home. Come to the brick yard tomorrow and I'll give you a job."

"If I'm too young to leave home, I'm too young to work in the brick yard," the boy spoke up.

Mr. Russell looked at him with narrowed eyes. "I ought to smack you for your impertinence," he said slowly, "but your remark has some basis in fact. You *are* too young to work in the yard or the coal mines or the clay works. You'd be in the way, or get hurt, or otherwise make trouble. So far that's been your history."

If his father had slapped him, it would not have hurt as much as those last words did. Charlie turned and ran to his room to seek consolation in his sketchbook.

Later his parents engaged a private tutor for him, but

this method of educating Charlie did not work either. When he was supposed to be studying, he drew pictures in his notebook or around the margins of his textbooks. Finally the teacher resigned.

"No one can educate such a mulish person," he said in disgust.

2

As the twig is bent

CHARLIE RUSSELL WAS BORN IN ST. LOUIS, MISSOURI, ON March 19, 1864, just at the end of the War Between the States, and the mold in which he had been cast was set by the time he reached twelve. He was a sturdy, stocky lad with straw-colored, stiff hair that he could never keep in place. His cheekbones were high, his mouth firm, and his square-cut jaw revealed a strong streak of stubbornness. He cared nothing about his appearance and his habitual untidiness was a source of constant distress to his mother. He had a mischievous, high-spirited nature that made him a ringleader among the other children but somewhat of a problem to his parents.

The Russell estate, on the outskirts of St. Louis, spread over many acres and included coal and clay mines and a brick factory, as well as a store, a school, a church, and houses for the laborers. It was, in fact, a small village in itself where Charlie often wandered about, getting acquainted with the Welsh workers and their families.

The property also included large vineyards, orchards, cornfields, and pastures.

The mines and factory were jointly owned by several Russell relatives and one in-law named John Parker; the business was called the Parker-Russell Enterprises and promised fine jobs for the male offspring of the families.

Charlie, like his brothers and numerous cousins who lived on the estate, had a wonderful childhood. He had his own pony, Gyp, and a small yellow dog named Tige. There were many fascinating places to explore without ever leaving the Russell land—especially a large wooded area known as Grandma's Woods, where the children loved to play Indians. There was nothing Charlie loved better than to gallop around among the trees and through the fields, yelling and slapping his mouth with his hand in imitation of the redman's war whoop. When they got tired of this game, they could always head for the small lake and go swimming or fishing.

There was no reason for a young boy to ever feel lonely or bored, but there were times when Charlie just had to get away and be by himself. At those times he would whistle to Tige, saddle up Gyp, and go off on an exploring trip. At those times he could pretend that he was out West—he was a hunter tracking down fierce wild animals, sleeping under the open sky . . . he was an Indian scout, riding the plains alert for "signs" that would tell him the enemy had passed this way, that they were just over the next rise . . .

His own vivid imagination, plus the waterfront tales

he eagerly listened to whenever he could, provided ample material for the adventure stories he spun out for his spellbound brothers and cousins, and served as the inspiration for many a rough-and-ready game he organized. Breaking the silence of a golden afternoon would come the blood-curdling yells and whoops of "savages"; peering around a rock or a tree could be seen the hideously paint-daubed faces of youngsters, chicken feathers rearing up out of their hair and sticks or clubs waving menacingly in the air. Casualties such as scraped knees and darkening bruises were to be expected, and the brave warriors wore their battle scars like badges of honor.

Charlie, too enthusiastic in the heat of one such battle, once brought his cousin Archie to the ground unconscious. He was terrified as he stared at the motionless figure; then he rushed over and held his cousin's head, pleading, "Archie, speak to me, speak to me!" It seemed ages before Archie's eyes opened and he gingerly rubbed the top of his head where Charlie's wild aim had landed.

Charlie gave a deep sigh and smiled at his cousin sheepishly, while all the other "Indians," considerably pale-faced under their war paint, decided it was safer to go hunting for bear, buffalo, and bobcats in Grandma's Woods. And indeed this game seemed much safer—until one day they wandered into the pasture during the "hunt" and were routed by a charging bull who resented their noisy intrusion.

The classroom seemed extraordinarily dull, the textbooks uneventful and boring, compared to the exciting adventures that awaited Charlie outside the schoolhouse.

He was never to lose his love of the out-of-doors and his interest in the colorful characters who *lived* the legend of the Wild West.

When he reached fifteen, Charlie found himself at loose ends in his small world. The cousins who were near his own age had gone away to school, but he had not finished the country school which they had all attended. The Welsh boys whom he had once played with were already working in the "diggings," so he spent most of his time drawing or painting or modeling wild animals out of clay or wax. His parents were proud of his skill, which they recognized as exceptional; however, they never seriously considered art as his lifework. When he was not drawing, he still spent his time along the waterfront.

He had grown fast the winter of 1878, but he was still stocky of build, as he would always be. Surely, he thought, he was tall enough now so that someone would give him a job which would take him to the land of his dreams. To his mind the most exciting and picturesque life was that of the buckskin-clad Indian trader. Such men had opened up the wilderness and they would certainly understand how a husky young lad felt about going West and seeking his fortune. But it seemed that the rough-looking men to whom he applied for jobs were not impressed by his eagerness and willingness to take any kind of work. The only response he ever got was a curt, "Can't use you."

Discouraged but still determined, he sought out his cousin Archie. "Let's go West," Charlie said.

"How'll we get there?"

"Run away. We'll hook rides when we can—walk the rest of the way. There are Injuns out in Montana, and cowboys. Life is too dull around here. Out there exciting things happen every day."

Archie, who had already fallen under the spell of Charlie's tales of adventure in the far West, did not need much persuasion to join in the scheme. Each boy packed a small supply of food and smuggled a small bundle of clothes out of the house. Carried over the shoulder on a stick, the sacks swung out behind the two boys in approved vagabond fashion. After walking for two days without getting a ride, each admitted to the other that he was weary and hungry and they decided to stop at a farmhouse to ask for work and a meal.

The farmer looked them over shrewdly, then a smile tugged at the corners of his mouth. "Runaways, ben't you?" he asked.

Charlie nodded.

"Got anything for a couple of young'uns to eat?" the man asked over his shoulder.

"Land o' Goshen!" the woman said. "Ask them in. Can't you see they're about to keel over from tiredness?"

"Come in and wash up then," Farmer Williams told them. "It's agin my principles to feed tramps until they've worked for their meals. But I'll make an exception of you. You can sleep in the loft of the barn, then bright and early you can get up and do the chores—feed the animals and chop and bring in wood. I'll show you how."

While they washed their hands and faces on the back porch, Mrs. Williams scrambled some eggs and put fresh bread and jelly on the table. Never had food tasted so good, and their bed of hay, they later agreed, was more comfortable than their own beds at home.

The farmer made the boys work hard and two days of it was all that Archie was able to stand. "Wherever we go we'll have to work like this," he told Charlie that night. "I've had enough. You can have your old West."

The next morning Archie set out for home. Charlie watched him go with a lump in his throat, thoroughly homesick himself but too stubborn to go back. He stuck it out for a full week before he finally told the Williamses that he felt he ought to go home, his parents would be worried.

"Well they might and they might not," the farmer said. "Maybe they're right glad to be rid of you."

"I don't think so," Charlie said. "I'm sure my mother must be worried."

Yet he wondered. Certainly he had never been any comfort to his parents. Although he had not done anything really bad, he knew that his failure to attend school or show interest in anything but art distressed them. Maybe they *were* glad to have him gone, but he must return and see.

After walking a few miles Charlie got a ride that took him all the way to St. Louis. It was evening when he walked into the Russell living room. His father was reading. His mother was playing the organ; Guy and Wolfert were singing. He stood in the doorway, expecting joyful cries of greeting. Surely his mother would jump up and throw her arms about his neck. But she only looked up and said, "Oh hello!" Then everyone went on with what he or she had been doing.

Guy finally turned and said casually, "Where've you been, Charlie?"

That was all. It was as though he had merely gone to a neighbor's for supper. A great lump rose in his throat. Weren't they even going to ask him if he were hungry? He was starving, but he was too stubborn to ask for anything to eat.

Turning on his heel, he went upstairs to bed, hungry and feeling very sorry for himself.

Later he learned that the farmer had sent word by a passing traveler to his parents telling where he was. His father had written back asking the farmer to keep him as long as possible and had paid the man for his son's keep.

3

Off to the land of his dreams

FOR AN ENTIRE WEEK CHARLIE STAYED AT HOME, CONtentedly drawing or modeling or taking long rides on Gyp, with Tige along for company. But gradually the old yearning to travel West took hold again. Surely life as a cowboy would be more exciting than his experience with the farmer had been. The two kinds of life were not similar.

Then, several days before Charlie's sixteenth birthday, Mr. Russell looked at the boy across the dinner table. "How would you like to go West, son?"

Charlie looked up cautiously to see if his father was joking; however, he seemed serious. His mother tried to smile but it was not very convincing, and Charlie thought that he saw mist in her eyes.

"How would I like it!" he cried, sitting up straight. "That's what I've wanted to do all my life."

"Well," his father went on with maddening slowness, "I've got a friend whose grown son, Wallis Miller—they call him Pike—has a spread out in Montana. A sheep ranch——"

"But I want to be a cowboy," Charlie broke in.

"Kindly let me finish what I was saying. In a few days Pike will be traveling to Montana. Since you're so set on going West, your mother and I will give our permission if you'll go with him. I hardly think you should be so particular about the kind of ranch it is, just so you are in the Wild West. And wild it is, I understand. Not only are the Indians still making trouble, but highwaymen and all sorts of rough characters make Montana their stamping ground."

"That's what I want to see!" Charlie cried.

"We're hoping, of course," his father went on, "that the hardships of that sort of life will make you realize what a pleasant home and a promising future you have here."

"But I want to *live* out West."

His father said, "Well, we can still hope that you'll change your mind before too long."

"Yes," his mother echoed. "We'll be hoping and waiting for you to come back. I can hardly bear to let you go."

Charlie did not tell her that he had been considering running away again as soon as he had saved enough to pay for food along the way.

In mid-March of 1880 Charlie set out to meet his destiny, plentifully supplied with pencils, paints, and modeling wax, which he stowed in stockings. He also remembered to pack several sketchbooks.

He and Pike were to go by train, and although Charlie was disappointed at first by this mode of travel, he soon found it exciting enough. Thanks to his father's generosity, he made the journey in one of the parlor cars, and there was also a comfortable berth available, which cost him seventeen dollars extra. Charlie was astounded by the speed with which the train ran: twenty miles an hour, day and night. It stopped to allow the passengers to eat meals at various stations along the way.

Besides the parlor car, there were other cars for second-class travelers. The seats were made of hard wood and passengers had to furnish their own bedrolls for sleeping.

After the train started, Charlie lost no time in wandering up and down the length of the cars several times to see what he could see. There were a few crinoline-clad ladies with full skirts in the parlor car, as well as a number of well-dressed men, many of them miners who had struck it rich and were going back to their "diggings."

In the other cars, however, were less prosperous but more interesting people, mostly men, who had exciting tales to tell of Injun scrapes, of bold highwaymen who held up stagecoaches, of cattle rustlers on the open range. Charlie hung onto every word they spoke until finally Pike in disgust told him that he was acting like a "hick," but Charlie ignored the remark.

As they moved further and further away from civilization, Charlie kept his nose glued to the windowpane, hoping for a glimpse of Indians or buffaloes, and on the third day out he did see a herd of shaggy animals. Indeed, he got almost close enough to touch them, for they crossed the railroad tracks and the train had to stop to let them pass. Filled with excitement, Charlie jumped off the train and ran up ahead to see this amazing sight. He could hear the animals snuff and snort and smell their strong odor. It took an hour for the great herd to pass; there were thousands of the shaggy beasts.

Later that same day he saw a small band of Indians—hunters, he surmised. He felt that he was in the land of adventure already. He sat up straight with excitement when the train pulled into a small station near Fort Hall and he saw the platform crowded with Indians, some with blankets, others in breechclout and leggings. He wanted to get out and take a closer look at them but was afraid to do so. Then, to his great surprise, as the train began to pull out, every one of the Indians clambered aboard, filling the cars. Charlie stared about in alarm, wondering if there would be trouble.

"Don't be scared," Pike told him. "When the railroad was built through here, the officials promised to carry the Injuns free of charge to any point on the reservation. They get such a kick out of riding on the 'iron horse' that they pile on every day and ride to the next station, then take the evening train back."

Charlie grinned and relaxed.

Charlie and Pike had to leave the Union Pacific Railroad at Ogden, Utah, and Helena, Montana, was still one hundred and fifty miles away. Boarding a bumpy, jerky, narrow-gauge railway that would take them to the Montana border, they headed toward the mountains. And one morning Charlie drew in his breath sharply as he caught his first glimpse of the high peaks looming up, white with snow, seemingly almost within walking distance.

After they reached the southern boundary of Montana, they had to travel on to Helena by stagecoach. It was raw and cold when the stage arrived; nevertheless, Charlie insisted upon sitting up beside the driver who told blood-chilling tales of being stopped by highwaymen or Indians. Perhaps he embroidered his stories a bit, but he was giving his young passenger many thrills, so they both enjoyed themselves.

"Perhaps you'd better let me handle your rifle," Charlie suggested.

"Do you know how to use it?"

"Oh yes! We hunted a lot in Grandma's Woods." Charlie didn't consider it necessary to add that the only game they shot was an occasional rabbit or crow.

The driver handed over the gun and Charlie sat with it on his lap, squinting his eyes to peer into the distance and searching each bush and rock they passed in order to spy any danger.

The driver looked at him and chuckled. "I doubt that we'll meet any hold-up men," he said. "I'm not carrying a payroll. But if we do run into trouble, I suggest that you just put up your hands peaceable-like when they tell you to. Most highwaymen have awful itchy trigger fingers."

There was no excitement, however, except the sight of buffalo herds and antelope. Pike and Charlie reached Helena with nothing more eventful having happened than a severe shaking up from the jouncing stagecoach, which had bumped like a bucking horse over the frozen roads.

Helena was later to become the state capitol; then it was nothing was a rough frontier town. Nonetheless, Charlie found it the place of his dreams. The stage driver had told him that in 1864 a party of miners, headed for the northwest, had chanced to find gold in a nearby gulch. The strike seemed so promising that a small settlement quickly sprang up and, unlike many such places, became permanent. Its founders called the village Last Chance Gulch, but its later citizens renamed it Helena. At the time Charlie Russell saw it, the town numbered around thirty-six hundred people.

The wide street was lined with crude frame shacks, which included several business houses and four saloons—the social meeting places of the motley crowds of men who flocked to the town from the mines and smaller settlements. The hotels and a few of the business houses were two-storied, but most of the buildings consisted of one floor with false fronts to make them appear more imposing. The sidewalks were made of rough planks; the single street was rough with frozen ridges now; Charlie could guess that in spring and fall it would be muddy and in summer ankle-deep in dust.

He noticed a few men wearing chaps and wide hats, but most of the people were rough-looking miners, with an occasional blanket Indian wandering the street. Disappointed that these Indians did not wear feathers and warpaint, Charlie was nevertheless excited by all the strange new things he saw.

Charlie enjoyed watching freight wagons come into town with a great clatter and creak of harnesses. The drivers shouted profanities at the slow-moving oxen; their sixteen-foot bull-whip lashes flicked out over the heads of the animals with cracks like pistol shots.

The place gave him a strange, exalted feeling. It was as though he had at last come home after long and weary searching. This country was where he belonged: he felt that with every fiber of his being. It was as though from the beginning of time he was meant to be in this region.

4

Helena and beyond

WHILE PIKE WAS BUYING PROVISIONS FOR HIS RANCH, HE and Charlie stayed at the International Hotel for the outrageous sum of two dollars a night. Their dinners in the large dining room cost seventy-five cents. At this rapid rate of spending Charlie was glad that his father had provided him generously with money.

When Pike went to buy two work horses, Charlie went with him and bought himself a mare and another horse. The man who sold them said that the animals could be used either for hauling a wagon or for riding. Charlie felt very important, being the owner of two mounts, and he was sure that Pike could not get along without him and his horses.

During their stay in Helena, Charlie spent most of his time wandering up and down, gawking at the leathery-skinned cowboys who strode about with an enviable air of self-assurance, their chaps flapping, their six-shooters strapped to their hips. There were also rough-looking buffalo hunters, but few women in this wild land.

One day he went shopping for his own western outfit, taking a great deal of time over each item he purchased. He bought blue jeans, leather chaps with huge silver *conchas*, a blue woolen shirt and fringed buckskin jacket with bead embroidery, a large hat and a red, blue, and green half-breed sash, such as the French-Canadians had worn on the St. Louis waterfront. He also bought a saddle, a revolver, a rifle in a bead-trimmed case, two blankets and a tarpaulin in which to roll them. Cowboy boots completed his purchases and nearly emptied his pockets. While he was changing into his new outfit in the hotel room, Pike came in.

"For heaven's sake!" he cried. "The Buckskin Kid in person. Just what do you think that get-up makes you?"

"A cowboy," Charlie replied calmly.

"But mine's a sheep ranch. You don't need any fancy rigging for that. Besides, there aren't more'n a couple of hundred cows in the whole territory of Montana."

Charlie pushed back his hat and scratched his unkempt hair in a gesture that became characteristic of him. "Someday," he told Pike, "I aim to be a cowboy. Someday there'll be more cows here than there are buffaloes now."

With those words Charlie Russell proved himself a prophet.

Before they left Helena they had dinner with two of Pike's friends, Colonel and Mrs. Ashley. After they had finished, the colonel and Pike went into an adjoining room to talk, while Charlie remained at the table to draw a sketch of a horse he had seen rearing in the street. Then he started to make a wax figure of the same horse.

Evidently the two men in the other room forgot that he was within earshot of their voices; nor was Charlie paying any attention until he overheard the colonel say, "Where on earth did you get that greenhorn kid? I never saw his like. His hair is so long and shaggy it ought to be sheared."

Pike chuckled. "I might do that as soon as I get hold of my sheep shears. He's a greenhorn all right—the most ignorant kid I ever saw."

From the first, Charlie had found Pike to be unpleasant and bossy; now he took a distinct dislike to the man. He felt very lonely that night as he went back to the hotel room.

Pike called Charlie before dawn the day they were to set out for the ranch, and leaving his warm bed so early in the morning was no easy task.

After calling the boy for the third time, Pike said impatiently, "You'd better crawl out now and in a hurry. I'm starting and I'd just as soon leave you behind as not."

Charlie's feet hit the floor with a thud. He had no wish to be stranded with practically no money in his pocket, even though he had a feeling that he and Pike were not going to get along very well. He gulped his breakfast and went out to help Pike harness the horses and saddle his own mount.

He felt excitement rise within him as they left Helena and headed east toward the snow-clad mountains and Judith Basin. He was facing a two-hundred-mile trip over rough, frozen roads, but at that moment the distance meant little to him, for at last he was in the land of his dreams.

They had not traveled far before Charlie, on horseback, sighted a herd of antelope skimming over the ground like the shadow of a cloud. His heart leaped into his throat at the sight. His enthusiasm dwindled, however, as the sun climbed higher and thawed the frozen ground, making it harder and harder for Pike's horses to pull the wagon. Finally Charlie had to hitch his two horses to the team and ride on the jouncing wagon. The cold wind seemed to penetrate through his heavy shirt, making him wish that he had bought a warm Hudson's Bay jacket instead of the foolish bright-colored sash he had tucked away in his bedroll. Ever since he had seen the French-Canadian boatmen with these sashes he had longed for one. Now that he owned it, he did not have the nerve to wear it in front of the scornful Pike.

Soon the going became even rougher as they came to a series of gulches and hills piled on hills. The first night out they slept in the wagon after cooking supper in the open. The food was too meager to satisfy Charlie's hearty appetite and he went to sleep still hungry.

Before nightfall the second day they reached the little mining town of Diamond City, where log cabins with sod-covered roofs huddled around the main building of town, the inevitable saloon. Charlie drank ginger ale and listened with eager ears to the tales of lucky strikes and claim-jumping, of bloody fights in the street and holdups by outlaws who robbed the miners of their pokes of gold.

The following dawn they started out along the west

flank of the snow-fringed peaks of the Big Belt Mountains and up through heavy timber and along the Musselshell River into the well-named Castle Mountains and Crazy Mountains. The scenes through which he passed etched themselves in Charlie's remarkable memory so well that he was able to reproduce them in his paintings a quarter of a century later—just as he was able to write the stories he had heard, using the same dialogue and told with such fidelity that readers were able to identify the men they depicted.

They slept with firearms close at hand, for Pike said there were Indians around who would be only too happy to make off with their horses and supplies. The threat of lurking danger lent spice to the trip, as far as Charlie was concerned. There was plenty of game to supplement their limited stock of food, and Charlie tried his marksmanship—with little success. Pike, however, was able to keep a fresh supply of meat on hand for their campfire meals.

After a few days the two travelers were aware of little but their discomfort as they bumped along mile after rough mile until it seemed that their teeth would be jarred loose. The sharp wind, blowing night and day, and rain mixed with snow made every hour miserable. Then at last, Charlie spied a pinpoint of light blinking ahead of them in the dark. "Must be a house," he called out, breaking a long silence. He and Pike had not found much to say to each other.

"Uh-huh. The Corrells—friends of mine. Most likely they'll ask us to stay overnight."

"That won't make me mad," Charlie said. "I could use a comfortable bed and some home-cooked food."

"You don't like my cooking?" Pike's tone was unfriendly. "If that's the case, suppose you do your own cooking from now on. And where did you think you'd find an extra bed in a one-room cabin? We'll have to spread our bedrolls on the floor."

"Well," Charlie said cheerfully, "at least it'll be warm and dry. I'm wet and chilled to my bones."

"Serves you right for buying a lot of fancy fixings instead of something sensible like a blanket coat. A lot of use you'll have for chaps on a sheep ranch."

The door opened as the team drove up in front of the little cabin. Charlie thought he had never seen such a welcome sight as that oblong of golden lamp light. A man stood in the doorway; and a young woman was peering over his shoulder.

"It's Pike, your neighbor."

"Light and come in," Correll invited.

Needing no second invitation, the two weary riders dismounted stiffly, stretched, and went inside.

"This is Charlie Russell, the Buckskin Kid," Pike introduced his companion. "How's the road to our ranch? I'd hoped to make it tonight."

"It's pretty bad," Correll told him. "You'd best stay here till morning. Susan, put two more spoons on the table and mix up some more biscuits."

While the woman was preparing the food, Charlie helped Pike unharness the horses, then hurried back again into the delightful warmth and delicious smells of the little cabin.

Supper consisted of stew and biscuits and dried apple pie, and for the first time since they had left Helena, Charlie had enjoyed a hearty and satisfying meal.

"Don't eat these people out of house and home," Pike told him. "Grocery stores are scarce around here."

William Correll smiled. "Eat all you want. There aren't any stores close by, but there's plenty of game. We're in no danger of starving."

That evening while the two men talked and Susan washed dishes, Charlie lay on his stomach close to the stove and on scraps of wrapping paper drew pictures of various animals he had seen on the long trip.

"Well, I declare," William said when he caught sight of the sketches. "I never saw such good drawings. You've got talent, young man."

Charlie was pleased and grateful. "Here, you may have them." Charlie handed the pictures to his host. "Perhaps I can pay for my supper this way."

Early the next morning Pike and Charlie thanked the Corrells for their hospitality and departed. By mid-morning they reached Miller-Waite Ranch. Jack Waite, Pike's partner, came out to meet them and help unload the supplies.

"I've brought us a new sheepherder," Pike announced as he got down from the wagon. "Jack, this is Charlie Russell, the Buckskin Kid."

Waite looked the newcomer over, his eyes lingering on the fancy chaps, but he said nothing. Charlie, noticing the smile that jerked at the corners of Jack's mouth, was not at all sure he was glad to have finally arrived at his destination.

It was not very long before Charlie found out what was expected of him on the Miller-Waite Ranch. He had to chop and carry wood morning and evening and wash dishes after meals. The rest of the time was spent herding sheep. He decided the very first day that he did not like the job. Among other things, the everlasting *"baa"* got on his nerves. Sheep were the most stupid creatures alive; furthermore, it was impossible to please either Pike or Waite. Both men found fault with everything he did or did not do.

There was only one good thing about the work: the sheep needed little watching, he thought, which left him plenty of time for drawing, painting, and modeling. The only trouble was, the sheep really needed more care than he gave them, for they had a habit of straying unless herded almost constantly.

When the two partners discovered that a number of their sheep were lost, Pike, in a rage, shouted, "You're the dumbest, laziest, most worthless kid I ever saw!"

Waite echoed Miller's sentiments in equally uncomplimentary language.

"If that's what you think of me, I quit," Charlie said with dignity.

"You can't quit," Pike roared. "You're fired."

Charlie was still trying to maintain his calm. "Give me my pay and I'll drift."

"Pay!" Pike was outraged. "You aren't worth the grub you ate. And you owe us for the lost sheep . . ."

Charlie decided that it was useless to demand money for his services, so he quietly packed up and rode away from his first job, which he had held for less than a month. Remembering his experience with the farmer when he had run away, he wondered if perhaps Pike had been making things difficult for him at his father's suggestion.

Oh well, he hadn't wanted to be a sheepherder anyway. He would find himself a job on a cattle ranch or find some other work. He would not return home defeated; nor would he write home for money—even though he knew it would be sent promptly. No, he had wanted to come West to make his own way and that's what he would do.

5

With Jake Hoover

NOT QUITE KNOWING WHERE HE WAS GOING, CHARLIE SET out on horseback, leading his other horse. His bedroll consisted of two Hudson's Bay blankets rolled around his precious paints, modeling clay and the clothes he had worn on his trip to the West. He stopped off at the Corrells' cabin; William and his wife had become his friends and he had paid them a few visits while he was working at Pike's ranch.

After Mrs. Correll had given him a good meal, William said, "The stock tender at the Utica stage station quit. Maybe you can get the job."

"I hope so," Charlie said. "I'll hurry right over there." He did not consider it necessary to tell the Corrells how desperately he needed that job.

But when he reached the station and applied for the place, the man looked him over and said, "You must be the greenhorn Buckskin Kid that Pike Miller told me about."

Charlie gulped and nodded.

"Can't use you," the man said with finality.

Miserable and discouraged, Charlie climbed on his horse and headed for the Judith River. Night was coming on, so he dismounted and hobbled his horses to graze. It was very cold and he had no food. Wondering what to do next, he built a fire and sat hunched beside it. He had never felt hungrier in his life, and it was not a comfortable feeling. He sniffed the air, thinking that he smelled food cooking . . . but he knew that it must be his imagination.

Suddenly a voice broke the silence: "Hello there, kid. What you doing here all by your lonesome?"

Charlie turned in alarm. There stood a shabbily dressed man, dimly outlined in the dusk.

Charlie tried to keep his voice from showing his fear. "I'm camping here."

"Where's your grub?" the stranger asked. He smiled and his expression was kind.

"Haven't got any."

"That's a bad state of affairs for anybody—especially a kid. Come on with me—I've got enough elk meat to fill up the hollow places you must have in your stomach."

So Charlie followed the man to the other side of some willows where a fire blazed merrily and meat was cooking in a skillet. While the boy rustled wood and brought a bucket of water from the river, the man added water and more coffee to the bubbling pot. The smell of coffee and frying meat filled the air and made Charlie feel that he couldn't wait until the food was ready.

He and his newfound companion sat on their bedrolls to eat, and never had food tasted so good.

"I'm Jake Hoover," the stranger said between bites of elk meat. "Hunter and trapper. Who are you and where you headed for?"

"I'm Charlie Russell. I was working for Pike Miller and Waite on their sheep ranch, but we had an argument and I left. I'm headed for anyplace I can find a job."

Jake shrugged. "Jobs are mighty scarce around here, but maybe something'll turn up."

"It better turn up fast. I'm broke. And I'm a long way from home."

He explained how he had happened to come West, then he found himself speaking freely of his hopes and ambitions, for Jake was a sympathetic and understanding listener.

After they had eaten, the hunter told Charlie about himself. He had been a prospector and miner and had staked out some rich claims, but some shrewd men had cheated him out of them. Now he trapped and hunted for a living, selling his furs at the settlement and his game meat to nearby ranchers.

"Any of those ranchers ever need a hired man?" Charlie asked.

Jake shook his head. "No one has more than a few head of cows—not more than he can take care of himself. I doubt that anyone could even offer you board."

"That's all I got at Pike's, and I nearly starved."

While Jake talked, Charlie studied him. He wore greasy buckskin breeches; his jacket was worn and dirty;

his dark, curly hair was shaggy. He was rough-looking, yet his blue eyes were gentle and his voice was soft and friendly. Already Charlie trusted and liked him.

Finally they spread their bedrolls and lay with their feet toward the fire. "Best keep your rifle close at hand," Jake said, "just in case. A fellow never knows when Injuns will show up."

For a long time Charlie lay staring up at the twinkling stars. What should he do now? What would become of him?

The next thing he knew, the sun was streaming into his face. Jake was already poking at the fire and meat was cooking in the pan, and again the tantalizing odors of boiling coffee and frying venison made Charlie's mouth water.

While they were eating Jake said, "I've been thinking: You've got no place to go—I get mighty lonesome up in the mountains. Why don't you throw in with me? Help me with my work and we can split the profits."

For a long moment Charlie was silent. There was a lump in his throat. It was as though he had been drowning and someone had cast him a lifeline. "Gosh! Thanks!" was all he could finally manage, but to Jake it was evidently enough.

"Good! We might as well get started. It's a long way from here."

As they traveled up into the mountains, the country became wilder and more beautiful with each mile, and a deep sense of contentment took hold of Charlie's spirit. Again came that feeling of being where he belonged.

Late in the afternoon, Jake said over his shoulder, "The Injuns made this trail when they usta travel into the high country to get hides for their clothing."

Charlie nodded. This would be the sort of country the Indians loved. The sun was setting and the loveliness of the rose and golden hues on the landscape filled him with the desire to get at his paints.

Finally they reached a park on the upper South Fork of the Judith, a grassy bowl surrounded by mountains, a scene of great beauty. Near a creek, almost hidden in a grove of aspens, was a cabin. As they approached it, the boy saw that it was actually two cabins with a space in between and a roof connecting them.

"I live in one room," Jake explained, "and I use the other to store hides and meat and my trapping gear. I built the place myself. There isn't a single nail anywhere —I used wooden pegs."

They removed their saddles and packs and hobbled the horses before turning them to graze. Then they entered the "living" cabin. Charlie's quick eye noted the dirt floor, a bunk bed in one corner with cedar boughs for a mattress. Two half-logs served as a table and the chairs were two stumps. The fireplace was used to heat the room and for cooking. At one end was a narrow window with a glass pane.

For the next two years this crude cabin would be Charlie's home. He was very happy, for he and Jake Hoover were kindred spirits. During that time he learned a great many things that would serve him well for the rest of his life.

Jake did not do any shooting near his cabin so the animals thereabouts were very tame and Charlie was able to sketch and paint them to his heart's content. He had no stomach for hunting or trapping; he loved wild animals too much to kill them. But he was willing to help Jake skin them, and this taught him the anatomy of various creatures.

The trips they took to the little settlements in Judith Basin and to the ranches were interesting breaks in the routine. The two partners kept busy, but Charlie also found ample time to devote to his art. He was delighted to find that Jake had a critical eye and could point out flaws in his work.

One day Jake said, "The first chance you get, you want to get rid of those big work horses and get yourself a couple of smaller ones—better for riding and traveling in this rough country."

A week or so later a band of Piegan Indians passed their camp. As usual, they were driving a small herd of horses. One of the animals appeared to be little more than a colt, but it caught Charlie's eye immediately.

"I want that pinto," he told Jake. "That's the horse I've got to have."

"Well," Jake replied as he slowly rolled a cigarette, "don't act so excited. I'll try to work out a trade for you, but don't let on you want that particular horse."

There was a great deal of jabbering and fingers flew while Jake traded Charlie's two big horses for two cayuses. Then he seemed to start dickering for a mouse-gray animal. The boy feared that his friend was not going to get the pinto for him, and never in his life had he wanted anything so badly. But finally, after much bargaining back and forth, the Indians rode away with Charlie's big work horses and left behind a gray horse and the pinto. The boy immediately named the paint horse Monte and the other one Gray Eagle.

"How did you do it?" he cried. "They acted as if they didn't want to give up the pinto."

Jake answered, "That's a mighty fine little horse you've got there. They never would have traded it if it wasn't what they call a ghost horse."

"A ghost horse! What's that?" Charlie asked.

"Well," Jake said, "here's what old Bad Wound, the pinto's owner, told me."

The horse had been a fine buffalo hunter. One day the Piegans got into a battle with some Crows and the young man riding the pinto was slain. When an Indian warrior died, it was the custom to kill a horse to carry him to the Happy Hunting Ground. So Bad Wound aimed his rifle and fired at the pinto. He thought the bullet had pierced the pony's head, for the animal fell to the ground and lay there motionless. However, the shot had only creased his neck, stunning him for a time. The next day Bad Wound saw the horse, his neck covered with dried blood, running with the herd. The Indian was frightened, for in his dreams he had seen his friend riding the horse to the Happy Hunting Ground.

"It's a ghost horse!" he had cried. "I will never ride him."

When he heard the story Charlie said, "I'm sure glad

Injuns believe in ghost horses. I've got me a fine mount. I'll bet he'll be the best horse in this part of the country."

He took off the jaw rope that the Indian owner had used and tried replacing it with a bridle and bit. Monte fought and Jake came over to help get the metal bar in the animal's mouth.

"I won't try to saddle him now," Charlie panted. "I'll ride him bareback."

He clambered onto Monte's back, but promptly was sent sailing through the air.

"Hurt?" Jake asked in concern.

"Nope—just mad." Charlie climbed on again and this time Monte did a jig on his hind feet. Charlie slid to the ground with a hard jolt.

"Take the bridle off," Jake suggested. "Put the jaw rope back on him and ride that way. You'll have to bridle-break him gradual-like."

Charlie followed Jake's suggestion. Then he mounted again and Monte did a lively sidestep that nearly unseated his rider once more. Charlie, however, soon had him under control and rode up and down before the cabin, letting the horse become accustomed to him.

When he climbed off, Monte again acted skittish, prancing sideways. "I know what's the matter," Jake said. "Injuns always mount and dismount from the right instead of the left."

"Sure enough! Well, I'll soon have him used to white man's ways."

He set to work with patient determination to train Monte with bridle and saddle. Before long the smart pony knew that Charlie was his master and he settled down to being the fine mount that Charlie had felt he would be. From then on, theirs was a firm friendship, lasting twenty-five years, until the pinto died of old age in a pleasant pasture.

As Charlie later wrote:

> Me and Monte were kids together. We grew up together, and were together for twenty-five years. When he died in 1904 I had ridden and packed him for thousands of miles. He was more than a friend to me. We didn't exactly talk together, but we sure savvied each other. Sometimes it seemed that he knew what was in my mind before I did.

One of his favorite pictures would always be one that he entitled "When I Was a Kid." It is a water color of himself on Monte crossing the mountains, Monte picking his way among the boulders followed by three loaded pack horses and Jake in the rear. It shows Charlie dressed in his fringed, beaded shirt with a fierce-looking knife tucked in his bright sash and a rifle in a beaded scabbard in front of him across the saddle. He had painted himself with a very severe expression, trying to look tough.

Although this is one of his earliest pictures still in existence—one that he did while living with Jake Hoover—it shows his remarkable sense of form and color and his natural ability as an artist of great promise.

Once Charlie had yearned for the life of a trapper such as experienced by Jim Bridger, Kit Carson, Joe Meek, and his own second cousin, William Bent. Such days were gone forever, but Jake managed to eke out a living of sorts by trapping beavers and muskrats and by selling deer and elk meat to settlers and selling or trading the pelts at Fort Benton. It was a rugged life, but Charlie thought it had been made to order for him.

Charlie saved every scrap of paper he could find for sketching. His parents would have been surprised to learn that their frequent letters, most of them urging him to come home, were as much valued for the blank sides as for the contents. White paper was hard to come by and furnished excellent sketching surface. The wild animals of the forest served as models, but Monte remained his favorite model, for he preferred drawing horses to any other creature.

One morning Charlie was alone in the cabin while Jake was off trading at the nearest settlement. After building a fire, he started to stir up some pancakes while the bacon cooked. Suddenly the sound of unshod hoofs outside reached his ears—it could not be Jake back so early, unless he had been riding all night. Besides, Jake's horses were shod . . . He opened the door and there stood a large fierce-looking blanket Indian.

"How!" Charlie said.

"How!" the Indian grunted. Carrying a rifle in his hand, he stalked into the cabin without invitation. He sat himself at the rough table and waved a hand toward the cooking food. Charlie understood instantly that he had a guest for breakfast.

It was a good chance to practice sign language, which

Jake had been teaching him. But the Indian seemed to be in no mood for conversation. He still wore his fierce frown as he began to stow away the food Charlie had been cooking for himself. There was no telling what to expect from any redman who might be nursing some secret grudge. Charlie forced himself to smile in a friendly manner, but his heart was pounding and he glanced toward his rifle resting on its pegs above the fireplace. His hunting knife was on a bench, out of reach. How he wished Jake would return! He was experienced in dealing with Indians, which Charlie was not.

As soon as the surly visitor finished eating, he wiped his mouth on the back of his hand and departed. After he rode off Charlie heaved a giant sigh of relief and hoped that he would have no more visitors.

After cooking another breakfast for himself, he smoothed out a piece of brown wrapping paper and drew a sketch of himself tossing flapjacks while the Indian watched him with a fierce scowl. He named this picture "Plenty Good Breakfast" and sent it to his parents.

Alarmed, his father sent money for him to come home. Charlie replied, "I'm earning my own money now. Soon I'll have enough saved to pay my own way for a visit. Thanks anyway." He returned the money.

Every letter he received from his parents contained the same question: *When are you coming home?*

"You oughta go," Jake told him. "After all, they're your folks. You won't always have them; someday you'll maybe be a lonely old codger like me."

Charlie looked up as his friend quickly. "You trying to get rid of me?"

"Not by a kettle full of beans. I'll miss you, you're swell to have around—not always airin' your tonsils like a lot of folks. You mind your own business and do your share of the work and are altogether mighty good company."

"Thanks, Jake. I reckon I oughta go home for a visit. The only thing is: They'll try to make me stay and work in the mines or make bricks. This is my part of the world, I belong here. I hate to disappoint my folks, but I'm going to come back. Now that they're bringing cattle into the country, I'd like to try my hand at being a cowboy."

6

To be a cowboy

IT WAS THE SPRING OF 1882 WHEN CHARLIE RETURNED to his home. He found the countryside a vision of loveliness, with the redbud and dogwood in blossom and many shrubs a lacework of tiny leaves. The air was fragrant and full of melody with the songs of birds. He had forgotten how imposing his home was with its great size and beauty of architecture. After Jake Hoover's rude cabin, it looked to Charlie like a palace.

The family, including all of the relatives who lived near or on the estate, flocked to welcome him and for days it was like a prolonged house party. At first Charlie enjoyed being treated like the prodigal son and it seemed that he could not get enough of Mammy Sukey's wonderful cooking.

However, before a month had passed, he was tired of the round of family gatherings, parties, gossip, and visiting the mines and brick works.

He had brought back the best of the drawings and paintings he had made at Jake Hoover's. His friends were impressed by the realism and the fine quality of his work.

His mother, from whom he inherited his artistic ability, said, "You undoubtedly have real talent, Charlie."

His father cleared his throat. "Fooling around with paints is, I suppose, all right as a pastime. But it's time for you to settle down and start making a living. Now that you've got this kid notion of going West out of your system——"

Charlie broke in, "But I don't have it out of my system. I'm going back. I'm going to be a cowboy."

"A cowboy!" both his parents cried out.

"What kind of fool notion is that?" Mr. Russell demanded. "You can step into a good job with a prosperous future right here. What sort of a future do you expect in being a cowboy?"

Charlie shrugged. At the moment he wasn't much concerned about his future. His square jaw jutted out stubbornly as he insisted, "I've got to go back."

There were many heated arguments between father and son. Charlie hated to disappoint his parents, but the idea of working at the plant still repelled him, and each day the call of the wide-open spaces became stronger. At last he was forced to blurt out, "I'm going out West again very soon, Dad."

His father said, "What's the matter with you, son? Here you can have everything you want. In time you'll be a wealthy man."

"I can't stay," Charlie said. "I don't know what it is about the West, but it's as if I belonged there . . ."

Mrs. Russell was bewildered by his attitude. "But from

what you've told us, it's such a crude, rough life. And you were reared so differently."

He put his arm around her shoulders. "I know you tried to civilize me, Mother, but I've got to go back. I can't explain it . . ."

Regretfully his father and mother accepted defeat. There was nothing else they could do.

Before he left, Charlie bought a large supply of paints, brushes, pencils, a fresh and bigger lump of beeswax, and a large supply of white drawing paper. He wanted to be sure he had enough to last him for some time; he was even taking a roll of canvas, for he hoped to experiment with oil paints.

Charlie had told such fascinating stories about the West that when he left, one of his cousins, Jim Fulkerson, went with him. At Billings, Montana, Jim came down with mountain fever and after a week of illness, died.

Charlie was stunned. Although he and Jim had not been close friends, it was a shock to him to lose one of his relatives, and the weight of responsibility was heavy on his inexperienced young shoulders. An uncle came out to accompany the body back home, but until his arrival Charlie had to make all of the arrangements. It took nearly all of the money both he and Jim had to pay the doctor and undertaker, but he did not tell his uncle about his financial straits. After paying the livery-stable expenses for Gray Eagle, Charlie found himself with less than a dollar in his pocket. He rode off wondering what would become of him now. He knew that he would be welcome back at Jake Hoover's cabin, but that was a considerable distance away. But as had happened to him before when he was broke and did not know where his next meal was coming from, Destiny seemed to take him by the hand.

Nearing Helena, he saw a string of horsemen and he decided to follow them. He saw them ride to the stockyards, so he rode over and asked one of the men who they were.

"We're a bunch of cowpokes come to get a thousand head of cattle for the 12 Z & V outfit in Judith Basin."

"What's the chance of getting a job?" Charlie asked, trying to act casual, although he felt that his whole future depended upon the answer.

"I dunno. Why don't you ask John Cabler, the boss?" The cowboy nodded toward a man with red whiskers who was shouting orders.

Charlie rode over and asked, "Any chance of getting a job with you?"

The man looked him over. "Had any experience?"

"I've done a lot of riding."

"Well, maybe you'll do as nighthawk for the horse herd. I had to fire the one we had—you couldn't be worse than he was."

Charlie knew that nighthawking was the lowliest job in the cattle business, but he was glad to get it. He would have to ride around the herd all night, until the regular herders got up. It was a solitary, dreary task and no one else wanted it. Yet he well knew what a great responsibility it was, for he and one other man were expected to guard and keep from drifting or stampeding the horses upon which the working of cattle depended.

A cowboy without his horse was a helpless and pitiable creature. Even the poorest cowboy had at least one horse upon which he lavished care and affection. Some of the wranglers had a string of up to a dozen saddle ponies, and their wealth was reckoned by the number of mounts they owned and the fanciness of their riding gear.

Strangely enough, Charlie did not mind his job, which most cowboys shunned. True, it was lonely work and the long night hours dragged, but he was self-sufficient enough not to mind being alone. He occupied himself with his own thoughts, and through his mind ran the daylight scenes of the roundup. Although he could not work with pencil or brush while nighthawking, he was busy planning the pictures he would make during his daytime leisure.

As the drive moved on slowly toward the Judith Basin, Charlie slept part of the day in the covered mess wagon as it bumped along. While supper was being prepared he worked at his sketch pad, drawing and painting. He gave his pictures away to anyone who admired them. He knew that his comrades considered him a little peculiar, yet he also knew that they liked him.

The time of day that he liked best was just before sundown when he and another cowpoke rode out to begin the night herding. By then the glare of the sky was softened and the slanting red rays of sunlight lay on the nearby hills and grassy swells, while a beautiful violet light veiled the distant mountains. Those rose and amethyst shades of evening and early morning appeared time after time in his pictures.

As he rode out, it seemed to him that he was entering a fresh new world of land and sky; all of his senses became keenly attuned to the sights, the sounds, the smells. He saw the land running on and on, without boundaries or end. He heard the horned larks and other gentle noises of evening. He breathed the fragrance of sage and wild flowers. Never had he been so aware of the hand of the Creator upon the world. As he rode circle in the deepening dusk, the shadows of the horses became ghostly and coyotes howled dolefully in the distance.

In later years he spoke of himself as being "not much of a cowhand." He did not go in for riding bucking broncos for sport. Being a good roper meant practicing throwing the lariat by the hour—time that Charlie preferred to spend sketching or painting. Yet he was conscientious about his duties and performed them well, knowing that he would be discharged promptly if he were careless. He very much wanted to make good at his job, for there were few other cowboy jobs available, and he would not consider having to ask his father for help.

Of course he knew he would be welcome back at Jake Hoover's, but he felt that it was an imposition to accept half of Jake's rather slim profits. Besides, it was a lonely life in the wilderness—here he enjoyed the companionship of a crew of friendly men.

He always got back to camp in the early morning just as the men were crawling from their bedrolls. The good smells of frying sowbelly and coffee filled the air. Some of the men were a bit grumpy at being wakened by the cook's banging on the dishpan with a large spoon, but they invariably perked up and smiled at sight of Charlie. At first he resented this, for he thought that the men were laughing at him; soon, however, he learned that they really liked him. He realized that there was something about his awkward gait, his too-large hat slumped over his ears, his ever-present lopsided grin, his way of making humorous remarks that cheered the men up, no matter how dreary the day. He stopped being annoyed when they teasingly called him their "camp jester."

Charlie was always famished when he first came in from night herding and he was likely to say after he had stowed away a huge breakfast, "I'm sure taking a big bite out of the boss' profits today." He usually stayed up long enough to watch the men rope and saddle their mounts for the morning's drive. Often the horses were "spooky," or nervous, early in the day and fought being saddled and ridden. Whenever one of the cowboys was unfortunate enough to be thrown, Charlie led the jeering. He was thankful that he did not have to saddle and ride one of those lively animals. Gray Eagle was not spirited enough to put on that sort of show. Charlie wished that he had Monte, who was spirited enough but well behaved.

To the others of the crew, the slow drive toward the Judith Basin was plodding and monotonous, but Charlie truly thought that he was living with a capital "L." He was doing a man's work and getting paid thirty dollars a month plus meals. It made him feel important to know that he had gotten the job on his own initiative and was holding it because he was doing his work satisfactorily. And there was always bound to be a certain amount of excitement during the day or night.

Some of the horses that had been ridden hard during the day were willing to graze quietly after the day's work and were not difficult to handle. Others might get "ornery" at any time and develop a yen to take off for home pastures or any other place. Then Charlie and his partner were hard put to quiet their charges. On stormy nights all the animals were hard to manage.

Many of the sights and events of that first big Judith Basin roundup were immortalized by his brush or pencil. One of his first sketches to become famous was one entitled "Rainy Morning." It showed the sodden earth, the men in yellow slickers trying to saddle reluctant horses. The camp wagon stood by the smoking fire where the cook was trying to get breakfast. The picture caught the dreary mood and showed, even in so early a work, his remarkable ability to arouse emotion.

Another of his pictures inspired by the same roundup was called "A Bronc to Breakfast" and shows a wildly bucking horse, with rider almost unseated, knocking over the coffeepot and kettles, while cowboys stampede out of the way of those flying hoofs.

The drive was necessarily slow, making only ten to fifteen miles a day, but finally the herd reached the Judith Basin, where the first large roundup was held. The cattle owners, who had but recently moved into

Montana, joined forces and the cattle were burned with the respective brands and regrouped in herds.

During the roundup Charlie got very little sleep. He was still required to night-herd the horses, but that duty did not prevent his helping with the branding. Here was exciting work that he did not wish to miss. He was not good enough at roping to toss a lariat from a running horse, but he was strong enough to help throw and hold down the bawling calves until the red-hot branding iron was applied.

With roundup over, it was no longer necessary to have such a large crew merely to hold the herd on the grazing ground. Men were being laid off. Charlie was worried: What should he do next?

Of course he could go back to Jake Hoover, as he intended to do as soon as possible, for a visit and to get Monte, but the thrill of being a cowboy had entered his blood. He did not want to settle down to the tame routine of being a trapper. He had never really liked the trapping business, but he had enjoyed Jake's company and he had had plenty of time to paint.

He hung around the camp a few days, hoping to be offered a job with one of the outfits, but one by one the cowboys who had not been hired as regular hands were drifting off, and finally Charlie drifted too. He headed Gray Eagle toward the hills where Jake Hoover's cabin was located, and like the other cowboys, he stopped for a meal and perhaps a sleep whenever he came to a ranch. He knew that a number of cowpokes spent the winter months drifting from ranch to ranch where they could be sure of a few meals and shelter for the night. Such cowboys were called "drifters," but Charlie had no ambition to be one of those.

Jake Hoover was delighted to see Charlie, and for a time the boy was pleased to be back, for the place had the feel of home to him. After sleeping on the hard ground, or jouncing in the camp wagon while trying to get some sleep, Charlie found the bunk bed, lined with cedar boughs, very comfortable indeed. Also, the leisure was welcome, for it gave him time to put on paper many of the scenes of the roundup that thronged his memory. And last but not least, he was happy to have Monte to ride again.

By autumn, life in the little cabin had become tame and monotonous for Charlie, and the more exciting life of the cowboy called to him. The long, lazy summer with Jake had given him time to think matters over and he knew what he wanted to do.

"I reckon it's time I was drifting," he said one morning at breakfast.

"You're more than welcome to stay, kid," Jake told him. "We can make a living at trapping and we'll do as we did before. I'll do the real trapping, since you don't like that part of it, and you can help me with the skinning and such. We'll split the proceeds. It ain't a fortune, but I make a good enough living."

"I know," Charlie broke in. "You've been mighty good to me and I'll never forget it. I'll always count you as one of my best friends. But my feet are itching to be on the move. Soon it'll be time for the beef roundup, and I ought to be able to get another job. I want to be a cowboy—I know that for sure now."

Jake nodded. "I understand how it is, boy, and you know you're welcome here any time."

So Charlie climbed on Monte, leading Gray Eagle as a pack horse, and set out for Judith Basin, where the large cattle ranches were located.

7

The stampede

ONE OF THE FRIENDS CHARLIE HAD MADE WHILE HE WAS with Jake Hoover was George Babcock, whom everyone called "Old Bab." His ranch was on the main trail to and from the Yugo Gulch mines and the town of Utica, so Charlie and Jake and everyone else who rode the trail always stopped there for a meal, a night, or several days. Charlie decided to spend a while there.

The day after Charlie arrived, Mr. and Mrs. Babcock and the hired hands made a trip to Utica for supplies, leaving their guest to keep an eye on the ranch. Finding a sack of dried apples on the back porch, he decided to make apple pies for the men to eat when they returned. He could not find any lard so he used bear grease for shortening. It seemed somewhat rancid, but there was nothing else available. The men came back late in the evening, having left Mrs. Babcock in Utica to visit friends. Charlie warmed up the stew he had made and served the men, giving them the apple pie for dessert.

The hungry men ate heartily but gave him no compliments on his cooking. That night they were sick.

Old Bab rose early and started out to get wood. He found his dog dead near the doorstep, evidently the victim of poisoned wolf bait.

"Hey Charlie!" he called.

Charlie came to the door and Bab pointed to the dead animal.

"You're a good kid and I like you," the man said with mock seriousness, "but when it comes to cooking—lay off. You make my men sick and kill my favorite dog."

During the day several miners and cowboys stopped off at the place and Charlie decided to stay over for another day and listen to the stories these men told. Later a man dropped in and he seemed to know everyone there but Charlie. The boy studied him in puzzlement—he was obviously not a cowboy or a miner.

When the man caught Charlie staring at him, he asked, "What are you looking at?"

"I'm trying to size you up," Charlie replied frankly. "You're either a preacher or a gambler."

The man chuckled and remarked. "You've got me figured out right." But he did not volunteer in which category he belonged.

Finally Bab introduced him as W. W. Van Orsdel, adding, "I don't savvy most of these psalm singers, but Brother Van sure deals square."

Charlie learned that Brother Van was held in high esteem by all who knew him and he later described this meeting and its effect on him in one of his famous letters:

Dear Brother Van:

I think it was about this time of year, 37 years ago that we first met at Babcock's ranch, in Pigeye Basin on the upper Judith. I was living at that time with a hunter and trapper, Jake Hoover, whom you will remember. . . . I had stopped for the night with Old Bab, a man as rough as the mountains he loved, but who was all heart from the belt up, and friends or strangers were welcome to shove their feet under his table. That all-welcome way of his made the camp a hangout for many homeless and prairie men, and his log walls and dirt roof seemed like a palace to those who lived mostly under the sky.

The evening you came, there was a mixture of bull-whackers, hunters and prospectors, who welcomed you with handshakes and rough but friendly greetings. I was the only stranger to you. . . . And when we sat down to our elk meat, beans, coffee and dried apples, under the rays of a bacon grease light, these men who knew little law, and one of them I knew wore notches in his gun; men who had not prayed since they knelt at their mothers' knees, bowed their heads while you, Brother Van, gave thanks, and when you finished someone said "Amen." I think it was the man I heard later was, or had been, a road agent.

I was sixteen years old, Brother Van, but have never forgotten your stay at old Bab's, with men whose talk was usually emphasized with fancy profanity, but while you were with us, although they had to talk slow and careful, there was never a slip. The outlaw at Bab's was a sinner and none of us were saints, but our hearts were clean at least while you gave thanks, and the holdup man said "amen."

You brought to the minds of these hardened men and the homeless, the faces of their mothers. A man cannot be bad while she is near. I have met you many times since then, Brother Van, sometimes in lonely places, but you were never lonesome or alone, for a man with scarred hands and feet stood beside you and near Him there is no hate, so all you met loved you.

"Be good and you will be happy," is an old saying which many contradict and say goodness is a rough trail over dangerous passes, with windfalls and swift and deep rivers to cross. I have never ridden it very far myself, but judging from the looks of you, it's a cinch bet with a hoss called Faith under you. It's a smooth, flower-grown trail, with easy fords, where birds sing and cold, clear streams dance in the sunlight all the way to the pass that crosses the big divide.

Brother Van, you have ridden that trail a long time, and I hope you will still ride to many birthdays on this side of the big range. With best wishes . . .

Your friend,

C. M. Russell

Charlie Russell set out from the Babcock ranch on a cold rainy morning. Old Bab urged him to stay until the storm was over, but he did not offer him a job.

"I'd better drift," Charlie told the man, "and see if I can't get me a job cowboying with Old Man True before he has his crew all hired."

As he rode he pulled his misshapen hat over his eyes to protect his face against the chill, driving rain. He turned up the collar of his yellow slicker to keep the rain from funneling down his neck, but the material from which the garment was made was too stiff to fit snugly and the rain continued to make him miserable.

When, after long hours of hard riding, he reached the True spread, he saw a group of men on horseback alongside a milling herd of cattle. Everyone was staring down at the ground. Charlie rode over to them and stood up in his stirrups to see what they were looking at. What he saw made him sick. Around the campfires he had heard of such things, but here was evidence of the most tragic sort of what could happen during a cattle stampede. The flattened forms on the ground had once been a man and a horse—he could see the remains of the saddle and the man's revolver. Someone was digging a shallow grave and what was left of the man was wrapped in his blanket and lowered into the hole.

Then, as the others bared their heads in the pelting rain, one of the men said the Lord's Prayer. Afterward, the same man said, "Back to your jobs, men. The cattle are still spooky and had better be held tight for a while."

Charlie recognized the speaker as the man everyone called "Old Man True," one of the prominent cattle owners of the region. The boy rode over and applied for a job.

"I was nighthawk for the horse herd for the Judith Basin roundup this spring," he said by way of recommendation.

"Of course," Nelson True said, "I recognize you now; you're Kid Russell. Do you want the job Hank had?" He jerked his thumb toward the freshly covered grave.

Charlie gulped but replied, "I want a job, any job. I'll do my best."

"I need another night herder," True said. "You just saw what can happen. The cattle have stampeded once—that means they will be ready to go again if you so much as blow your nose or light a match."

"I know that," Charlie said, "but I'm not afraid. My horse, Monte, has more sense than most men. He'll keep me out of trouble."

"Even a smart horse is apt to step into a prairie-dog hole in the dark," True went on. "Being smart won't help either one of you then."

Charlie gave the man his famous lopsided grin. "I know. But I reckon this outfit has had its share of bad luck for the season."

"I hope you realize what a great responsibility will be on your shoulders. You're pretty young and this is a man-sized job I'm giving you. My cattle and horses are my fortune."

Charlie nodded soberly.

The man went on. "The Piegans consider this their hunting ground. Although they're supposed to be on the reservation, they consider it their right to leave any time they feel like it, and stampede and steal livestock. The rustlers are just as bad. Your job is dangerous and important—the safety of my property is in your hands."

One of the more experienced hands, Nate Grimes, was to be Charlie's partner on his first night out.

"You know," Nate said as they rode out, "it's the

custom for night hawks to sing to the horses or cattle they're herding."

Charlie chuckled. "If they hear my frog-croaking voice they'll high-tail it to the nearest timber."

"Animals aren't very particular. You just sing slow and kind of soothing-like. It makes them feel easier and lets them know where you are so that it won't spook them when you suddenly loom up in the dark. You'll want to put your yeller slicker on because the nights are cold. And, if the horses or cattle should happen to stampede, for gosh sakes, keep on singing. So will I. That way, we'll both know the other one is all right."

Charlie thought that first night would never end. He had forgotten how monotonous it was to be riding around and around in a circle. His bones ached and it was difficult to keep awake. When his croaking voice became hoarse, he settled for humming, but decided to learn more songs from the other men. Finally soft gray tinged the horizon, then gradually turned to pink, and at last it was time to drive the horses to camp where the cowboys roped the ones they were to ride. Charlie dismounted and turned Monte to graze, giving him an affectionate pat on the rump.

He shuffled up to the covered chuck wagon where "Gladys" or the "Old Woman," as the men called the man cook, was holding forth, dishing up flapjacks, bacon, beans, and coffee. Charlie stumped along, stooped over like an old man crippled with rheumatism. "Oh, my aching joints," he moaned, but his face wore a crooked grin. "I'll give a plugged nickel to anyone who'll rub me with axle grease."

Then he whisked an envelope from his pocket and quickly sketched a picture of an old man bent over, leaning on two crooked sticks.

"I aged awful fast last night," he said, passing the sketch around and bringing forth a laugh from everyone.

Things went well with Charlie for some time as the herd slowly approached the Judith Basin. Then one night the weather turned foul, with thunder booming and lightning zigzagging across the sky. The horses became restless, and when the flashes of light showed up the landscape Charlie could see that the nearby cattle were restless too. Their horns rattled and fingers of lightning danced on their tips.

A brilliant flash of lightning and a terrifying blast of thunder seemed to rip the heavens wide open. Horses neighed, the longhorns bellowed—then everything on four legs started to run.

Charlie put heel to Monte's ribs, pounding forward to get ahead of the herd. He remembered to sing at the top of his voice to let Nate know where he was. He realized the possible danger of Monte's stepping in a prairie-dog hole and throwing him beneath those thundering hoofs. He also remembered the smashed corpse that was being buried the day he came to ask for a job. Yet there was no easy or safe way to do what had to be done. He had to take his chances.

Monte, seeming to know what was expected of him, raced alongside the panicked animals and seemed to be gaining. When Charlie saw by a flash of lightning that he was near the head of the herd, he guided Monte to press against the lead horse, but this seemed to have no effect upon the stampeding beasts. He knew there was a deep gully ahead. Unless the herd was turned before it reached that place, the creatures would plunge to their death.

Charlie drew out his revolver and fired. That did the trick. The lead animals swerved to the left and finally they all began to mill about in a circle until they tired.

It was then that Charlie remembered that he hadn't heard Nate's voice for some time. He did not dare yell lest he frighten the animals again, so he sang at the top of his voice: "Oh, Nate my boy, where are you? Oh, Nate my boy, let me hear your voice so true!"

There was no answer. Charlie continued to sing, but he sang alone, his heart pinched with fear. Nate would have answered, he would have been singing to the horses, if he were safe. Charlie shuddered as he visualized the trampled body of his partner.

Morning dawned with the air feeling fresh and clean after the storm. Downhearted, Charlie rode toward camp, this time with no humorous quip for the cowboys. Instead, he would be the bearer of sad tidings. His head hung low on his chest and even Monte jogged along dispiritedly.

Suddenly he heard galloping hoofs coming up behind him and Nate rode up. Charlie stared at him. "You—you're all right?"

"Sure I am."

"But where were you? I couldn't hear you singing; I didn't see you when it began to get light."

"Oh, I high-tailed it for the hills when the herd started to run. I remembered how poor Hank looked after the herd trampled him. I didn't like the idea—it's such a messy way to die."

Charlie looked at him with contempt.

"If you tell the boss, I'll slit your throat," Nate told him, his dark eyes gleaming.

Charlie did not answer. He was not afraid of Nate's threat; obviously the man was a coward. He did not relish the idea of being a bearer of tales, yet he did not want to night-hawk with this man any longer.

Before he could decide what to do about the matter they reached camp and Nelson True was striding toward them. "Last night after the stampede I was riding around to see if all was well," he said. "I heard only one man singing to the *remuda.* And if I'm not wrong it was Russell's frog croak I heard. Where were you, Nate?"

"Oh, I lost my voice temporarily," the man said glibly.

The boss did not look convinced. "Charlie," he asked, "did you at any time pass Nate while you were riding the circle last night after the stampede?"

The boy heaved a sigh of relief. All he had to do was to tell the truth; it was not necessary for him to tattle. "No, I didn't," he answered.

"That's what I thought," the boss said curtly. "Nate, right after breakfast I'll give you your time. Then get on your horse and drift."

8

The long drive

CHARLIE'S FRIENDS CALLED HIM "KID RUSSELL" AND SPOKE of him as being a maverick; that is, an unbranded calf that did not fit into any particular classification. He would always remain an individualist whom everyone liked. Although his shabby manner of dress made cowboys smile, his grin and personality were so engaging that people instantly became his friends.

During his waking hours, when he was not busy with his sketching pad, time did not hang heavy on his hands, for there was plenty of excitement in camp. Every bit of prairie and meadow and draw had to be searched for miles around and the longhorns all driven into a great loose bunch before the work of separating began.

In the open-range days the cattle during the winter drifted for many miles and the animals belonging to various ranchers were all mixed together. For the sake of economy the cattlemen joined forces, appointing a range boss who had absolute authority over the cowboys. Then each rancher sent cowboys to represent his interests. After the big roundup the calves were branded with the mark of the cow it was following. Branding, Charlie thought, was an exciting part of the cattle work. He never tired of watching the cowboys rope the bucking calves, then throw them to the ground. Well-trained cow ponies held the rope taut while the hot iron was pressed against the calf's rump. Often Charlie took a hand by sitting on the head of the calf during the branding.

The smell of sweat, dust, burning hair and flesh, never ceased to excite him. To him, the life of the cowboy contained more thrill and drama than any other occupation, even though he had no aptitude for the special cowboy skills that made a top hand. In spite of the fact that he had grown up practically on the back of his own pony, he was not a good rider. He was sure that Monte was the best and smartest horse in the outfit, but he did not train his pony to cut out a certain animal from the herd and keep it from rejoining the bunch.

He was satisfied to be a nighthawk, for this gave him time to gaze at the colorful Montana sunrises and sunsets: the purple, gold and rose tones that tinted every hill and valley. He especially liked to watch for the soft velvety grays of dusk and the golden pink of dawn that ended his long, lonely night rides.

More and more he was learning the habits and anatomy of cows and horses and he frequently drew out his sketch pad to make note of some special detail. And, although he did not know it then, he was living through a most dramatic chapter of American history, which he would effectively record later for posterity.

When Charlie first went to Montana in 1880 the

territory was practically uninhabited. He and Jake had often traveled for many miles without seeing a dwelling of any kind, whereas thousands of buffaloes darkened the plains and antelope, deer, elk, wolves, and coyotes were plentiful. Three years later, there was not a buffalo to be seen and the other animals were scarce—but there were six hundred thousand head of cattle grazing on the range and the colorful cowboy with his chaps, clanking spurs, wide hat, and gay neckerchief had come to stay.

Charlie knew the man who started the cattle business in Montana. It was Granville Stuart who in 1860 bought some lame oxen from immigrants at Fort Hall for a small sum. He trailed them into Montana, fattened them, then drove them back to Fort Hall the following summer to sell or trade for more lamed animals. The market for beef at the nearby mines was excellent and the new industry grew fast. In 1866 Nelson Story drove in six hundred head of longhorns over the Bozeman Trail. The Texas trail drives had started.

In a few years, overcrowding became a problem in western Montana, and when Granville Stuart drove the first herd into the central part of the territory, the cattle business really began to boom. Grass was free. All a cattleman had to do was publish in the nearest weekly newspaper that he claimed a certain piece of land, setting various hills, rivers, buttes, or draws as boundaries. He also published his brand. It was all so simple that there were many times when Charlie wished he had enough money to buy a small herd of cattle. He would not have to buy land to run them. Indeed, the land, being unsurveyed, was not for sale and most cattlemen owned not even the ground upon which they built their dwellings.

As the spring roundup of 1883, the biggest in history, drew to a close, Charlie again wondered what he was going to do. The cows would drift until the beef roundup in the fall and he did not have a steady job cowboying with any outfit. To his surprise, however, Nelson True asked him to work as night rider for his cattle herd. True was one of the most prominent pioneer cattle barons of Montana and his asking Russell to work for him meant that the boy had made good.

The man said, "I try to keep my critters from drifting all over the range during the summer, so that it isn't such a job getting them together in the fall. I've noticed that you're a good night herder. I'd like to hire you."

Charlie grinned. "I'd like to work for you."

"You don't mind night-herding?" True asked, giving Charlie a piercing look.

The boy shrugged. "I know I'm not any great shakes as a cowboy—ropin' and ridin' and such. But I'm fairly good at singin' to the herd."

There were more dangers to contend with night-herding cattle than there were with horses, for the cattle were more likely to stampede during a bad night. Furthermore, the Indians had acquired a taste for beef and had developed the trick of snapping a blanket on a dark night in order to set the herd into a stampede and thereby catch a stray or two.

The Piegans especially thought that the Judith Basin

was their own hunting ground, but the Crows were also in the habit of making raids in this region. One morning Charlie and his partner came across a small band of Indians engaged in skinning a steer they had killed.

"Let's ride on and pretend we don't see them," suggested Charlie's companion. "They've got us outnumbered, and the steer's dead. Nothing we can do about it."

"Naw. We've got to scare 'em or they'll get the habit of slaughtering True's animals. Put up your rifle and look fierce."

The two riders went galloping up to the Indians who grabbed their own guns. There were women and children with the small band, and they were obviously hungry. Charlie had considerable sympathy for the Indians, who had been driven from their own lands onto reservations and made to adopt a way of life foreign to their nature. Many cowboys shot Indians caught in the act of stealing or of slaughtering stolen cattle, but Charlie Russell was not one with a nervous trigger finger.

All that he and his companion did was make a fierce show of anger and shout and wave their rifles and gesticulate toward the carcass and toward the ranch-house. Charlie, who had learned some sign language from Jake Hoover, guessed from the signs of the men in the group that the steer had been brought down by wolves that they had driven away. They were merely making use of the meat that the wolves would have eaten.

"Not kill our cows! Never again!" Charlie shouted with a fierce frown, also using what signs he could remember.

The Indians must have gotten the gist of his remark, for they shook their heads emphatically and said, "No! No!"

"Let the poor devils go," Charlie said. "We've scared them enough so that I think they'll leave True's critters alone."

As soon as he had time, Charlie used this incident as the subject for a picture which he called "Caught in the Act." His boss saw the picture and admired it.

Pleased, Charlie said with a grin, "It's yours if you want it."

"I'd like to hang it on my wall," Nelson True said.

Charlie's grin widened. "I've got a bunch of pictures stowed in my war bag that I'd like to have you keep for me until I have a place for them, if you will."

Later, True looked over the drawings and paintings and observed, "I'm no artist but these look good to me. It seems that I have a cowboy-artist in my crew."

"I like to draw and paint," Charlie explained modestly. "Fact is, I've got to mess around with pencil or paints or modeling clay or I ain't happy. But I realize that work like that don't buy any beans. I won't forget that you're paying me to be a cowboy."

Old Man True nodded his approval. "But it seems to me that your art work is good enough to be published. I saw some pictures by someone called Remington in *Harper's Weekly*. Your work is just as good—if not better. Do you object if I send some of your pictures to the magazine?"

"Of course not," Charlie said, never dreaming that anything would come of it.

In spite of True's good intentions, several years went by before he got around to submitting Charlie's work. But when he finally did, he surprised Charlie a few weeks later by handing him a slim envelope. In it was a check for ten dollars for his picture "Caught in the Act."

Charlie stared at the check unbelievingly. "You mean they paid me good money for a picture?"

"It appears that way," True said. "Read the letter."

"They write," Charlie said slowly, "that they'd like to see more of my work."

It had never occurred to him before that art might be a way for him to make money.

Later he received a copy of the magazine containing his picture. The comment with the illustration read:

> Mr. Russell, the artist, has sketched a subject with which he is entirely familiar. The starving Indians, with savage faces . . . The gaunt, sore-backed horses humped by the cold . . . the scurvy dogs, snarling at the scent of blood-drops in the snow. Mr. Russell has caught the exact dreariness of it all . . . Anyone acquainted with frontier life will at once appreciate the truthfulness of the picture.

Charlie's first year as a cowboy was a busy one. In the fall he worked as nighthawk during the beef roundup in which the animals to be shipped to market were gathered together. Then he went along on the overland drive in which the thousand steers were driven over the long trail to the Northern Pacific Railway, where they would be loaded and taken to Chicago.

Thus far, this was the largest herd of cattle shipped to market. The crew was equipped at Utica, with Nelson True in charge, Hatch Tuttle as foreman, and Mike Shannon as the "Old Lady," or cook. Frank Plunkett was Charlie's partner as night herder.

There were eight cowpunchers, a trail boss, a horse wrangler, twenty-five horses and the chuck wagon. The men slept in their bedrolls and ate a steady diet of beans, corn meal, molasses, sugar, coffee, with dried apple sauce as a special treat now and then. Breakfast was at daylight, after which the herd was allowed to graze for a while. When the horse herd and mess wagon had pulled out ahead, the cattle were started with two men in the lead as "point." The other men rode at the sides, with two at the rear as "drag" drivers. This historic trip lasted two months, during which time Charlie learned much about the ways of cattle, horses, and cowboys.

When they passed Indian tribes, Charlie immediately made notes of their colorful dress and the distinguishing features of their faces. He could scarcely wait to get what he had seen down upon his sketch pad. The drive furnished subjects for several pictures, notably "Deadline on the Range" and "The Hostiles."

Near the head of Swimming Woman Creek, Charlie saw the corpses of seven Crow braves, lying as they had fallen in death, and was told that they had been on a horse-stealing expedition against their ancient enemy, the Piegans, but had been defeated.

After finding this gruesome evidence of the warlike mood of the Piegans, True turned his drive toward the southern projection of the Bull Mountains, trying to avoid the tribe. They followed the Yellowstone River in the direction of what is now Billings and made camp near Pompey's Pillar, a landmark famous since Lewis and Clark came upon it in 1805. Charlie laboriously carved his name in the huge sandstone rock.

The herd had to pass through the Crow reservation where the Indians halted the drive and demanded a dollar a head for allowing the animals to pass. This was the Indian custom called "taking toll," an incident that Charlie later commemorated in a picture by that title. True, however, refused to comply with the Indians' demand and ordered that the herd be driven down the river to ford at Terry's Landing, whereupon the angry Crows flapped their blankets and shouted in an effort to stampede the animals. Fortunately, the cowboys were able to prevent them from doing so. Charlie, on Monte, eagerly joined in the excitement, although he was required to do only night-herding.

Getting the cattle into the water was a difficult task. Charlie "hi-yi-ed" as loudly as the rest of the cowboys. The Indians added to the pandemonium by continuing to yell and flap their blankets. Actually, however, their efforts helped rather than hindered the efforts of the crew.

Finally the lead animals were forced into the river and the rest followed, but when the swift current hit them mid-stream, they turned and tried to come back. The cowboys redoubled their efforts and at last the longhorns pushed steadily toward the opposite shore.

The sight of two thousand head of cattle bobbing in the swift water was such an exciting scene that it took Charlie's breath away, but he knew that he would be unable to capture it with his brush.

Only a few head of cattle were drowned in the swift-flowing river. "I got off better than I expected," Nelson True said. Then he turned to Charlie and added, "You'll do to ride the river with, my friend."

Charlie flashed a pleased grin as his thanks. He knew that this was the highest praise a cowboy could receive, for swimming a herd across a swift river was dangerous business and most such crossings cost a life or two.

That was the only really dangerous incident during that long, slow drive. They had to travel slowly in order to allow the cattle to graze, for the idea was to put weight on them rather than take it off. Fortunately there were no serious stampedes, which not only were dangerous to man and herd, but took poundage off the cattle—and pounds meant money at the market.

At the railroad Charlie helped to herd the bawling steers into the cattle cars, and afterward rode to Chicago as a "cowpoke." He learned then that this term was meant quite literally, for during the trip it was his duty to walk along the top of the cattle cars and with a long pole prod the animals that had fallen until they rose to their feet. When the train stopped, he and the other cowboys got out and walked along the sides of the cars, continuing to poke at the fallen beasts.

When they reached Chicago his companions headed for the nearest saloon but Charlie set out to explore the city. In a very short time he was lost and during his wandering among the crowds of people he felt lonelier than he ever had in his life. He finally had to ask a policeman to direct him back to his hotel near the stockyards. He had had enough of the city and already yearned for the wide-open spaces, but his cronies still had some celebrating to do.

His roommate was Hatch Tuttle. Charlie went right to his room, exhausted, but after he had been in bed a short time he felt that he was suffocating. He had tried to raise the window but could not budge it. He threw aside all of the covers but it did not help.

Finally Hatch Tuttle said, "I'm stifling! I can't stand it—I've got to have air."

"Me too," Charlie responded. "I'll break the darned window and pay for it in the morning."

He got up, picked up his boot, and with it smashed the glass where he saw a streetlight reflecting upon it.

"That's better," Hatch said, breathing in audibly.

"Yeah, it sure is." Charlie climbed back into bed and gratefully drew in deep breaths of what he thought was fresh air. Both cowboys then fell instantly asleep.

In the morning Charlie was awakened by a loud whoop. He sat up in bed and stared about in bewilderment. Hatch, doubled up with laughter, was pointing to some broken glass in a bookcase. "There's the 'window' you broke to let in fresh air," he said.

Charlie looked over at the window which was still shut. "Well, I'm a maverick's uncle," he said, brushing the shaggy lock from his eyes. "Here I thought sure I was breathing in cool air. Reckon as long as we thought so, it doesn't make any difference. I guess we both slept. At least I did when your snores didn't wake me up."

9

First romance

THE ELEVEN YEARS THAT CHARLIE RUSSELL SERVED AS cowboy on the Montana range in Judith Basin were the most hectic and turbulent days of the state's history. That time marked the subjugation of the Indian and the rise of various bands of outlaws; rustlers and bandits who finally met their downfall during the Vigilante Days.

He saw the beginning of the open range when Judith Basin and the surrounding country became booming cattle ranches and the ranchers made incredible sums of money. He also saw, and was made unhappy by, the small settlers who came in, set up homesteads near the best water holes, and fenced off their acres by barbed wire. He recognized this as the end of the free and open range. Would it mean the end of the days of big ranches? he wondered. Would the range become broken up into many small outfits?

The coming of the railroad was the biggest single factor in bringing about the change in the way of life. On September 9, 1883, the first trainload of passengers drew in to Helena—an event that ushered in the beginning of the new era. With the railroad came families of settlers, schoolteachers, merchants, preachers, lawyers and others who symbolized civilization. Montana would never be the same again.

About a thousand hide hunters were busy during 1883-84 killing the buffalo, the mainstay of life for the waning tribes of Plains Indians.

By 1884 the depredations of cattle rustlers were reaching alarming proportions and many cattle rustlers had become adept at changing brands on cows. It was all too easy to brand and claim any calf found wandering on the open range. As Granville Stuart later wrote about a nearby settler:

> Near our house we discovered one neighbor whose cows invariably had twin calves and frequently triplets, while the range cows in that vicinity were nearly all barren and would persist in hanging around this man's corral, envying his cows their numerous children and lamenting their own childless fate. This state of affairs continued until we were obliged to call around that way and threaten to hang the man if his cows had any more twins.

Horse thieves were viewed with even more hatred than cattle rustlers. On the plains a man's horse meant his very life, for on foot no one could long survive in a blizzard. Even on horseback the distances were so great that a man could easily starve to death before he reached a place where he could get food.

Finally matters reached a point where the ranchers felt forced to take the law into their own hands. In those days there was little actual law enforcement on the frontier, and such justice as citizens administered was likely to be sudden and effective, usually permanently. Under the leadership of Granville Stuart and Angus Fergus, an armed vigilante force of about one hundred and fifty cattlemen and cowboys were organized to seek out and punish the bold, lawless men of the region.

Although he had no personal conflict with them, Charlie knew that the numerous bands of outlaws all were united by bonds of mutual interest and protection. Among the many hideouts and places where they gathered, there was one in the Judith Mountains which was known as "the worst place in Montana Territory and the resort of outlaws and thieves." Billy Downs, a trader, used his store as a supply source for men of shady reputation, most of them notorious horse thieves. They would drive their stolen livestock into the Badlands, alter the brands, then sell the animals along the Missouri or in Canada, where they would steal more horses and drive them to booming Montana Territory to sell. Such dens of known thieves the Vigilantes had taken oath to wipe out. The members were sworn to secrecy, but such information is bound to leak out. Although Charlie liked adventure, he took a definite stand against killing, so he refused to join the Vigilantes. He was well aware, however, that no fewer than twenty-one men were captured and hanged from the gallows tree in Hangman's Gulch.

Such was the exciting atmosphere in which Charlie Russell spent his late teens. The Vigilantes continued to operate against the badmen of Montana, and served to make rustling and horse-stealing risky, but the evils were slow in being wiped out entirely.

Troubles between the white men and the Indians were also intensified as more and more settlers came into the country. The cowboys, too, added their share of excitement whenever they went into town. It was their custom to ride up the single street shouting and shooting to liven things up.

Charlie didn't miss much of the excitement and it is told that he often did his part in "livening things up." At the same time, however, he was soaking up every impression, every event, every change. He never forgot the things he saw, and later his paintings and sketches proved to be a pictorial record of the times, documenting in an unforgettable and enduring way the wealth of frontier lore.

After Charlie returned to Judith Basin following the cattle drive, he decided that he would take up a homestead, build a little cabin, and maybe set up a cattle business for himself. He well knew that his father would be glad to loan him the money to start. In fact, it was his parents' fondest wish that Charlie stop drifting and settle down. But he stubbornly refused to ask for aid.

He selected a homestead in Pigeye Gulch, not far from Utica, the center of Montana's cattle activities. There was water nearby and it was close to timber which, with the help of Monte, he could snake in. He set to work with great enthusiasm to build a cabin before winter set in. As the job progressed, however, it became apparent to

Charlie and all who saw his cabin that he had no talent for building. The logs were of different lengths and different circumferences. The walls were crooked and before he got them high as his head he grew tired of the work and decided to put on the roof, which consisted mainly of brush. He made a circle of rocks in one corner of the room and designated this his "fireplace."

Jake Hoover rode over for a visit when the cabin was finished. "Why didn't you make a chimney?" the trapper asked.

"Oh, there's plenty of cracks in the roof to draw the smoke out," Charlie drawled. "Don't need a chimney."

"Evidently you don't need a bed either," Jake pointed to a pile of brush with a blanket thrown over it. He chuckled. "And I guess you haven't any use for a table or chairs or anything else so luxurious."

"Nope. This is plenty fancy for me. Oh, in time I might haul in a couple of logs to sit on and get me a stump to use as a table. But I don't like things too fussy—makes me uncomfortable."

"Well, any time you get tired of roughing it, come up and see me. There's always plenty of elk meat and a welcome for you," Jake said as he rode off later.

Charlie's lopsided cabin amused all who saw it, and many of his friends rode a considerable distance to view the strange dwelling. It added to young Russell's growing reputation as an eccentric and helped to build the legend that was accumulating about him.

He liked the place, however. It was the first spot that had ever been entirely his own and it was also his first studio. Here on the stump he had dragged in to use as a table he made many sketches and paintings of the things he had seen during the exciting months just passed.

Charlie was also winning a growing reputation as an artist among his friends, but he painted because he *had to,* not because he had any serious intentions of using his talent to make a living or even add to his earnings. He gave away most of his art work or used the pictures to pay grocery bills. Sometimes this sort of payment was accepted reluctantly, the new owners not realizing that someday Charlie's art work would be of great value.

Soon after he built the cabin, which became the joke of the countryside, Mr. Edgar, a wealthy neighbor of the Russells in St. Louis, came West to set up a ranch in the Judith Basin. He had two pretty daughters and girls were scarce in the valley, so it was not long before numerous cowboys were spending most of their spare time at the newcomers' ranch, Charlie Russell among them. Because he was acquainted with the parents, he had an advantage over the others and the Edgars encouraged his visits. His main reason for going was the older daughter, Lollie.

When another girl came to visit the daughters, there were many social affairs in her honor: dances, picnics, horseback rides. Charlie was included in most of them and he became so smitten with the charming Lollie that he went so far as to take a bath and shave and put on a clean shirt every time before he called upon her. He even had his shaggy hair cut.

He always took along his latest picture to show her.

"You have a real future as an artist," she told him one day.

Her parents echoed her views. One evening when he was dining with them Mrs. Edgar said, "Why don't you go back East to some good art school and really settle down and become a first-class artist? You certainly have talent."

"Shucks!" He grinned in bashful modesty. "Drawing and painting is just a pastime with me. I like to do it—just as I like to do things such as this."

He showed them a figure which was an extremely good miniature head of Mr. Edgar. While he was talking, his hands had been busy fashioning the little figure from the lump of wax he always carried in his pocket.

"You *are* clever!" Mr. Edgar exclaimed. He looked at Charlie appraisingly for a long moment, then said, "I agree with you, however, that art is a precarious way to make a living. I presume that you will soon be going back to St. Louis and entering into your father's business. Art can, of course, continue to be your hobby."

"Nope!" Charlie said, his square chin firm. "I don't aim to go into my dad's business. I like it too well in this neck of the woods."

There was a long, uncomfortable silence. Then Mrs. Edgar asked, "But what do you intend to do out here? I mean, by way of making a living?"

Her questions made Charlie painfully aware of the fact that he was at present unemployed. He cleared his throat. "I've been thinking of going into cattle ranching on my own," he said.

"That sounds like an excellent idea," Mr. Edgar said enthusiastically. "I'm sure that your father would be glad to back you financially . . ."

"Oh no!" Charlie broke in. "I wouldn't ask my father for help. He was sure that I'd do just that—or go back, defeated, to beg for a job. But I aim to fool him. Nope! I'll get along on my own."

Again an uncomfortable silence fell. Charlie realized, of course, Lollie's parents had been pumping him for information about what he planned to do with his future. Obviously they were becoming alarmed over their daughter's growing interest in him. Lollie's cheeks were pink as she broke in with some inconsequential remark in an attempt to change the subject. The conversation became general and Charlie relaxed.

But from that time on Charlie noticed a chill in the Edgars' attitude toward him. Evidently they had ceased to look upon him as a desirable suitor. Charlie, when he looked at his lopsided shack and considered his lack of prospects, did not blame them, so he decided to give Lollie up. But three days away from her was all he could stand.

He slicked himself up and saddled Monte and rode over to the Edgar ranch carrying a roll of his latest drawings. Mrs. Edgar came to the door.

"I came to see Lollie," he said with his bashful grin.

"I'm sorry, but she isn't here."

"Where is she?"

"In St. Louis. She won't be back. We've sent her to a girls' school."

"Won't be back?" His voice was stricken.

"I'm sorry," she said again. Then when she saw the expression in his eyes she put a hand on his arm. "It wouldn't do," she went on kindly. "You know it wouldn't. You'll get over it . . ."

Charlie stumbled away from the doorstep, sure that he would never get over his love for Lollie. And he carried her memory in his heart for a long time.

"That Lollie girl sure caught this cowpoke in her loop," he often said to friends. "I like to never got over her."

10

A fork in the road

Charlie began to spend more and more time with his paints, and decided to try the oil paints he had brought back from St. Louis. This new medium fascinated him even more than water colors had and he often rode up to Jake Hoover's place so that he would have more room and leisure to experiment with oils. He was driven to do more paintings by the knowledge that the West, as he knew it and loved it, was dying and he felt impelled to portray the changing ways upon canvas.

During the year 1886-87 that Charlie worked for the Stadler-Kaufman outfit, he realized that the range was rapidly becoming overstocked and that there was no way to prevent it. The grass was free and a man could drive in as many cows or sheep as he was able to buy.

Hatch Tuttle said to Charlie one day, "A hard winter or a dry summer would bring disaster to all this whole range."

Charlie nodded seriously, not knowing then that his friend was speaking as a prophet. That winter was mild and dry and the spring rains did not come. Many cattle died from eating poisonous larkspur, which they browsed on when grass was scarce. The drought continued through the summer, with the heat soaring to 110 degrees in the shade day after day. As the brassy sun continued to blaze, the parched land became a vast tomb, with heat waves shimmering over the sun-baked plains. Hot winds licked up every drop of moisture and shriveled the grass. It was, Charlie and the others knew, perfect weather for prairie fires.

Then one afternoon what everyone had been fearing happened. Charlie and Hatch were out driving a herd of cattle to new feeding grounds, when suddenly the younger man straightened and rose in the stirrups as he peered into the distance.

"Hey, Hatch!" He pointed to the west where a wide plume of smoke stood out plainly against the faded sky. Both cowboys knew instantly what it was and what it meant. That prairie fire could devour the dry grass at a rate of forty or fifty miles an hour—faster than cows or even horses could run.

"There's only one thing to do," he shouted to his partner. "Kill one of Stadler's fifty-dollar steers, like he told us to, and drag the carcass over the flames."

Tuttle nodded, his face set and grim. Without delay his rope snaked out and caught a steer. Charlie jumped from Monte's back, whipping out his knife as he did so. He quickly slit the critter's throat. By now they could feel the heat, hear the flames crackle. A high wind had come up and the fire was racing across the plains.

Monte neighed shrilly and started to prance. "Whoa there, boy," Charlie said soothingly. "I'm depending on you." He knotted the ends of reins together and put them over one arm.

Charlie and Hatch cut the head from the dead steer and split the carcass lengthwise. They made two fire drags by putting the split sides down. Each fastened ropes to the fore and hind feet, then rode at a brisk trot on each side of the speeding, low wall of fire.

This method was effective in putting out the worst of the blaze. By this time other cowboys had arrived with wet sacks and blankets to beat out any sparks or outbreaks fanned by the wind. Blazing embers of dry cow chips or clumps of grass were blown ahead of the burned-out line and the men fiercely fought the flames until sunset, when the wind finally died down. In spite of the quick work of every man available, a hundred acres of precious grass had burned.

The exhausted men rode back to camp. Earlier, even the cook had been helping to fight the fire, but when things got pretty much under control he went back to the chuck wagon and by the time the men straggled in he had dinner ready for them: blanket steaks (steaks rolled in flour and cooked slowly in a covered kettle), baked potatoes, stewed tomatoes, and biscuits with molasses.

Although Charlie thought he was too tired to eat, the smells from the kettles gave him an appetite. After he had eaten, some of the weariness eased from him, but he said, "I reckon I won't be going to any dance tonight."

Stadler announced, "You men better get rested up fast. Tomorrow we start a drive to new feeding grounds. There isn't enough grass left around here to satisfy the rabbits."

At dawn the next day they began what turned out to be a long, terrible drive. Charlie was still blinking with sleepiness when he came to the chuck wagon to pile his plate high with biscuits and beans. "That," he said with a yawn, "was the quickest night I ever spent."

He was sent out to ride left flank, near the rear of the herd. Because the ground was covered with ashes that rose in choking clouds, Charlie tied his bandanna over his nostrils and his mouth. He also tied an extra handkerchief over Monte's nose, and the horse seemed to understand that his master was trying to relieve his discomfort. Smoke still blanketed the land. The sun, still a blurred ball of fire, had lost none of its intensity. In spite of the covering on the lower part of his face, Charlie could feel his skin was becoming parched and cracked. His eyes smarted and watered.

As they moved along through so much desolation, it seemed to Charlie that the land he loved was changing, dying before his eyes. Would it ever be beautiful again? The bawling herd moved at a crawling pace; each mile was like a league, each hour an eternity. Just when Charlie thought that he had reached the end of his endurance, he noticed that the cows had raised their heads and were stepping more briskly.

They must be nearing a river. Now the cattle smelled

the water and broke into a run. No power on earth could stop them. Charlie did not try. He reined Monte to one side of the herd as the thirsty creatures raced by bellowing. Across the Judith River, the grass was more abundant and water was nearby, so camp was set up on the opposite side.

Although the brassy sun continued to blaze and there was no relief from the heat, the cattle were driven back to the home range in late August in fairly good shape for the winter—if it was not too severe.

In the early fall, however, Charlie noticed many wild animals moving southward. The ducks, wild geese, and songbirds also departed earlier than usual and the cows began to grow shaggy coats. For the first time he saw white Arctic owls come to Judith Basin. While riding one day he came across an Indian camp, where an old Indian pointed to one of the owls sitting on a fence post. "Heap cold winter. Brr!" he said, hugging himself and shivering. He went on to tell Charlie in sign language that he had not seen white owls since he was a boy and that had been just previous to a terrible winter.

On the sixteenth of November there was a severe storm and the temperature fell to two degrees below zero, with a strong wind blowing. Eighteen inches of snow fell and in places it was whirled into deep drifts.

Charlie and the other cowboys piled on all the warm clothes they owned and went out to try to keep the cattle from drifting against the barbed-wire fences or into coulees where the drifted snow had created dead ends. He bent his head against the blinding particles of snow, but he still found it difficult to keep his eyes open. As the wind roared, the cattle hunched their backs and turned tail or drifted before it.

That first storm caused some loss of cattle, and the stockmen prayed for the chinook: the warm wind that usually came upon the heels of a storm to melt the drifts and snow so that the animals could get at the grass. But the chinook did not come. There were two more bad blizzards in December; then in January it snowed an inch an hour for sixteen hours without stopping. And still there was no warm wind. Snow fell intermittently for another ten days.

"There won't be a critter alive on this range unless a chinook comes in a hurry," Charlie said to Hatch as they were putting on two suits of underwear and everything else they could find before going out to do what they could for the starving, freezing livestock. They also wore socks over their faces with holes cut out for their eyes.

Hatch nodded, saying nothing. The cowboys' spirits were as low as the stockmen's these days. There was no hay to feed the animals. Stadler had managed to buy some straw, but it served only as stuffing, for it had no nourishment. All that Charlie and his fellow workers could do was to try to prevent the cattle from drifting, or drive them into some fairly sheltered draw, or pull them from drifts. It made Charlie sick to see all the stiff carcasses lying about in the snow. He was sure that this winter would mark the end of the open range, as indeed it did.

Icy air stabbed into his lungs as he rode and there

were times when he wondered if he would make it back to the ranchhouse. He was well aware that a number of cowboys had given their lives while carrying out their duties. He had always prided himself on his sense of direction but one night during a blizzard the wind and snow hit him with such fury that he literally could not see his hand before his face and he finally had to admit that he was lost.

"Whoa there!" he shouted to Monte and it seemed to him that the wind ripped the words from his mouth and hurled them away to nothingness. Monte, however, responding to the jerk on the reins, stopped. Charlie tried to peer into the swirling clouds of snow but he could see nothing. It looked to him as if he were riding the body of a headless horse.

"Steady, Charlie old boy," he told himself. "You mustn't panic now. Use your head."

In the intense cold his limbs were stiffening, so he climbed down, intending to walk and lead Monte. But he could make no headway against the terrific wind—in fact, he could not even keep his feet. He drew the pony around to shelter himself from the full force of the blizzard, keeping the reins hooked over his elbow, and began to stamp his feet and swing his arms to get the blood to circulating. Only when he felt that, for the time being, the danger of freezing to death was past, did he climb into the saddle. He jerked the right rein, thinking it was east—the direction of the bunkhouse—but Monte tossed his head and refused to obey. No matter how hard Charlie pulled on the lines and pounded Monte's ribs with his heels, the horse would not go in the direction Charlie was guiding him.

"Well, old boy," Charlie said, "I reckon you may be smarter than I am. Truth of the matter is—I'm lost. Completely."

He eased his hold on the reins, gave Monte his head, and the horse plowed determinedly forward. After they had been going for an interminable time Charlie muttered, "I hope you know what you're doing, fellow. I still have a feeling we should be going in the opposite direction . . ."

Soon, however, he did not much care. He felt a warm and delicious drowsiness creeping over him . . .

The next thing he knew he was in the bunkhouse, lying on a blanket on the floor in front of the stove. Several cowboys were rubbing him with snow.

"Hey, what do you think you're doing!" he protested.

"Shut up!" Hatch told him. "We're trying to thaw you out—trying to save your worthless life. That's all."

"He'll make it now," Jesse Phelps said. "Wrap him in blankets and put him in his bunk."

The thawing-out process was so painful that Charlie did not feel much like talking for a while, but after the blood was once more circulating through his veins he asked Hatch what had happened.

"That Monte horse of yours," Hatch replied, "not only brought you here to the bunkhouse, but he kept whinnying until we finally heard him above the wind."

"Monte's a darn sight smarter than I am," Charlie admitted. "I'd be frozen stiffer than a plank out there by now if he hadn't of known the way home. I hope you gave him some extra fodder."

"I sure did," Hatch told him.

Now and then someone on horseback was able to reach town to buy supplies and bring back the mail. Charlie and the others derived small satisfaction in reading the newspaper dispatches:

Omaha: It has been blowing a blizzard since early this morning and every railroad is more or less blocked. Travel is entirely suspended. The storm is general throughout the plains region.

Sioux City: A train with 100 passengers on board is snowbound eleven miles west of Canton, Dakota. The Milwaukee railroad is lined with engines in drifts.

Denver: The westbound Kansas-Pacific mail train has been snowbound at Brookville since Monday. The eastbound train, delayed at Hugo, is expected through tomorrow. No Burlington train has arrived since yesterday.

Sioux Falls: More snow has already fallen than during the entire of last winter.

The weather was terrible throughout the entire West, but central Montana got much the worst of it. The thermometer dropped to 42 degrees below zero. The snow remained crusted over, piled in deep drifts so that the cattle could not paw through to reach what scant grass lay below.

Charlie and the other cowboys worked until they were ready to drop, cutting down trees and brush so that the starving cattle could gnaw the branches and bark. What little hay there was had to be taken out by toboggan and scattered to small clumps of cows. The memory of those cruel months would live in Charlie's memory for the rest of his life.

One day Jesse Phelps, foreman of the Stadler-Kaufman outfit, received a letter from Louis Kaufman, who was in Helena, asking how the cattle were doing. Phelps shook his head sadly. "I suppose," he said, "I'll have to write and tell him how tough things really are. I sure hate to do it but I'll have to break the news that he's wiped out."

Charlie was sitting at the table with Phelps and some of the other men. "I'll make a sketch to go with your letter," he offered. He took a small piece of paper out of his pocket and, getting his paints, swiftly did a water color of a single cow, hardly more than a standing hump-backed skeleton, with coyotes waiting nearby for the animal to fall. The cow bore the Bar B brand on its hip. In the lower left-hand corner Charlie drew a buffalo skull with his initials. Later he used this symbol of the dying Old West as his personal trademark on all his pictures. Charlie labeled the water color "Waiting for the Chinook."

Phelps put it in an envelope and mailed it without a letter. There was no need for words. Although it was a rather crude piece of art hastily done, it graphically told the dreadful story of that fateful winter of 1886.

Kaufman was so impressed that he showed the painting to all his friends and later had it printed on postcards and sent them all over the country. However, he called it "The Last of 5000," and this title was retained on the first Russell picture to bring fame to the artist.

Recognition had been slow in catching up with Charlie Russell, mainly because he had not sought it. But that small picture caught the public fancy, and more and more notice came his way. Jesse Phelps asked him to do a painting of the Utica cow camp. The foreman was well pleased with the picture and asked Charlie how much he wanted for it.

Charlie hemmed and hawed, scratched his head, and finally said, "I reckon ten dollars would be about right."

"I'll give you twenty dollars and consider it a bargain," Phelps offered. "And I'm going to enter it in the St. Louis Exposition for you. It might win a prize."

The picture did not win a prize, but it was accepted for exhibition and Charlie later heard that his parents and relatives viewed it proudly. Several of the relatives wrote asking him for paintings, but did not offer to pay him. He generously sent a number of his earlier works for distribution to those who had been kind enough to express admiration for his work.

James R. Shelton also commissioned him to do another painting of a Utica cow camp, and he, too, doubled the ten-dollar fee. It made Charlie feel foolish to take so much money for doing what he liked to do.

About this time a newspaper reporter arrived from Helena and, after seeing some of Charlie's pictures on view in the local saloon, asked for an interview with the cowboy-artist.

In the January 12 issue of 1887 the following item appeared in the *River Press*:

> While at Utica a *River Press* representative met Mr. Charles M. Russell, an artist of no ordinary ability. He had painted several of the most spirited pictures of cowboy life we had ever seen. . . . Mr. Russell prides himself on being a cowboy and has engaged in the business for several years. . . . Mr. Russell is a natural artist and we have been informed that he never had any instruction . . .

A month or two later, Jesse Phelps told Charlie that he had sent another picture to be put on exhibit in a store window in Helena. "Your work is good enough to be seen by a lot of folks," Phelps said. "It wouldn't surprise me if you get to be famous one of these days."

Charlie grinned at him. "Maybe I can get more suckers to give me twenty dollars a picture."

"You might be able to ask a lot more than that," Phelps replied.

The foreman had an I-told-you-so expression on his face when he handed the cowboy-artist a clipping from the Helena *Weekly Independent* for May 7, 1887. Charlie read:

> A COWBOY ARTIST
>
> *A Fine Oil Painting by a Range Rider Who Never Studied Drawing in His Life*
>
> On the wall in Huntley and Pruitt's store hangs a painting with a strange history . . . if slightly inartistic in some of its details, [it] is of fine conception and, in the

main, finely colored and executed. It was painted in the seclusion of a cow camp on the Judith Range, and by a cowboy. It represents a roundup camp, scattered out on the range after early breakfast—the boys saddling their unruly cayuses, the vicious beasts bucking in every conceivable shape or flying away towards the herds. The foreground shows the camp-fire, tents and mess wagons, and in the background stretches a range of mountains. . . . Altogether it is a wonderfully faithful picture and one that bears much study. The artist is Charles Russell, a cowboy 21 years of age, the son of a well-to-do family of St. Louis. He is a natural artist but never had a day of study in that line. . . . The cowboy life suits his eccentric nature, and especially night herding, at which his time is spent. . . . Russell it was who painted the realistic picture of ravaged desolation entitled "Waiting for a Chinook," which has been extensively photographed.

"What you ought to do," Phelps advised him, "is take a batch of your paintings to Helena and put them on display in various hotels and store windows. They'll be bound to attract attention. You might make some sales."

"I'm nothing but a cowhand and not a very good one," Charlie protested. "Why should I put on airs of bein' an artist?"

Phelps persisted, "You *are* an artist, my friend. And I never knew anyone less given to putting on airs. You take my advice and go to Helena."

Charlie had been well enough satisfied with the thirty dollars a month he received as a cowboy and he loved the life; but between seasons when there was no work for him, he had a hard time making ends meet. The extra forty dollars he had earned on his two sales to Shelton and Phelps had been most welcome.

He began to think seriously about taking some of his pictures to Helena. He might make a sale or two; and anyway he needed art supplies. He finally went and had no trouble at all in finding merchants who agreed to display his pictures, provided they got 10 per cent of the price if any sales resulted.

The day after his pictures were put on display in store windows Charlie was visited by a reporter of the Helena *Weekly Herald.* Two evenings later he unfolded the newspaper and read the following account of himself in the issue of May 26, 1887:

A DIAMOND IN THE ROUGH

> Within twelve months past the fame of an amateur devotee of the brush and pencil has arisen in Montana, and, nurtured by true genius . . . has spread abroad over the Territory.
>
> Seven years ago a boy of sixteen years left his home in St. Louis and came to Montana, going into the Judith Basin, where he got employment on a cattle ranch and has remained ever since. . . . The spark of artistic genius, implanted in his soul, soon made itself visible and called his energies into the cultivation of talent and ability for sculpture and painting. . . . The young cowboy employed his leisure in modelling figures out of plastic material and in transferring to canvas and paper representations of the crude scenes surrounding his life. . . . Never having taken a lesson and with nothing to guide his pencil but the genius within him, C. M. Russell became

celebrated in the neighborhood as a painter. . . . [His] forte lies in depiction of animated scenes . . . all drawn from his Montana life on the range and their faithfulness is surprising.

Charlie chuckled when he finished the article. "I reckon I ought to go out and take a look at that picture," he said to himself. "That fellow must be good."

He strolled down the street and stopped at the store window where the picture the reporter had praised so highly was on exhibition, along with six more of his paintings. Several people were standing there and it was obvious from their remarks that they were well pleased with what they saw. It amused him to mingle unknown with these people who were talking about his art. He noticed one distinguished-looking gentleman who was scrutinizing the central canvas with unusual interest.

"Seems to me," Charlie drawled, "that the artist fellow, whoever he is, daubed on the rosy-lavender paint a mite too thick."

"Oh no!" the gentleman protested in a shocked tone. "It's wonderful! Truly wonderful! I have seen the land out here in Montana look just that way in the evening. That mauve light lays over the landscape just like that. I have never before seen such life, such realism, in a painting."

Charlie suppressed a chuckle and drawled, "You must think the artist is good."

"He's extraordinary!" the man said emphatically. "He has unusual talent. I read that he had no training whatever. I must have that picture in the center, and several of the others. I must meet the artist, I must talk to him."

Charlie hesitated a moment, then extended a hand. "Well, sir!" he said. "The man is close enough to you. I'm Charlie Russell."

The man gasped, then gripped the extended hand. "Where can we go to talk?"

"My hotel is only a couple of blocks from here," Charlie replied. "I reckon that's as good a place to talk as anywhere."

The two fell into step together and the stranger introduced himself as Mr. T. W. Markley, from Washington, D.C., on a visit to his son, A. W. Markley of Helena.

When they were seated in the dingy lobby of the hotel, Mr. Markley told Charlie that, as a patron of the arts, it was his pleasure in life to discover and aid talent. After questioning Charlie and learning that his formal art training had lasted for less than a week, he sat forward in his chair.

"You must go to the best art school in the country—then to Europe. I will pay all of your expenses. Talent such as yours must be developed to the fullest. The best school is in Philadelphia . . ."

Charlie was dumfounded. He had hardly expected anything like this. He didn't know what to say.

Mr. Markley became impatient of the long silence. "Of course you'll accept my offer?"

Finally Charlie managed to answer, "I—don't know. I'll have to think it over. Make arrangements . . ."

"Of course." The man smiled genially. "I realize what a surprise such an offer is. Make your arrangements and let me know when you are ready." He handed Charlie a card with his Washington address and left.

Charlie lay awake long into the night thinking about the unusual offer. Did he really have such exceptional talent? He knew that something within him made him draw and paint and mold wax figures. He would be miserable if he could not do these things. And men like Mr. Markley—who obviously knew a great deal about art—were willing to pay good money for things he had done merely for the love of doing them. Was it his duty to "develop his talent to the fullest"?

He loved the wild, free life of the West. He had no desire to go to some center of civilization to study art. He was satisfied with doing the best he could with every picture.

He finally fell asleep still pondering the matter. He slept fitfully and woke unrefreshed, with Mr. Markley's offer still uppermost in his mind. If he accepted the offer, it would change his life completely. Did he want his life changed? He had been well pleased with it as it was, even though he was not making much money. But making a lot of money had never been important to him.

Certainly, though, he had come to a fork in the road. Which turn should he take?

11

A serious question

THE NEXT DAY CHARLIE LEFT HELENA AND WENT BACK to Judith Basin to deliberate his problem still further. As he rode he passed a small band of reservation Indians, shabby, dispirited, hungry-looking. Perhaps they were on their way back to the reservation after visiting relatives; since there were women along, it was doubtful that they had been raiding some cattleman's herd.

He thought about the sad lot of the Indian in comparison with the wild, free life of his former days. With the coming of the white man, the Indians had been driven from the choicest lands and their means of livelihood, the buffalo, slaughtered. They were no longer "the noble redmen," but abject creatures dependent upon the honesty or whims of their reservation agents.

Charlie had now and then toyed with the idea of spending some time with a tribe of Indians, to study them and their way of life; but their existence on the reservation did not interest him. The only Indians that he knew who lived in a primitive fashion were the Bloods, cousins to the Blackfeet, who dwelt in Canada.

Previously this had been but an idle thought indulged in as a daydream—as he rode along now deliberating on whether or not to go to art school, the idea seemed not too farfetched. This was something he ought to do *before* he made his decision. If he went to study art for several years, it would be too late by the time he came back—if he ever did. The Bloods, too, would eventually be driven onto a reservation.

When he got back to Judith Basin he tried to get a job at one of the ranches. Things were in a sorry state. All of the cattlemen had suffered heavily during the previous winter and jobs were scarce. He spent some time "line riding," that is, drifting from ranch to ranch getting a few nights of free bunk and board at each place. Then he visited Jake Hoover for a while, but found life there too monotonous and lonely.

Returning to Helena to put on display the paintings he had done at Jake's, he ran into two cowboy friends, Phil Weingard and Bob Stillwell. While celebrating their reunion at the hotel, Charlie spoke of his desire to spend awhile living with Indians.

"I hanker to live like a redman," he said. "In the old-style way. I want to sleep in a tepee and live off the land just like the Piegans and the Crows and the Blackfeet used to do around here."

Weingard said, "I always did reckon you were part Injun—with your high cheekbones. If you had dark hair you'd look like one."

"I really mean it," Charlie went on seriously. "I've got a problem to solve and I believe I could think things out real well in a tepee. Anyway, I want to try that kind of life before the Canadian Injuns get shoved onto reservations. Why don't you fellows come along?"

Before the night was over the idea appealed to all three of them.

The next morning Charlie's brainstorm still seemed a good one and the trio made ready to set out. Part of their preparations consisted of Charlie's and Weingard's going to a photographer and having their picture taken in Indian garb—Weingard as a painted warrior holding a gun across his lap—Charlie, wearing a frowzy black wig, posed as his squaw.

By the time the three reached Alberta, Canada, Weingard and Stillwell's enthusiasm for the project had evaporated. Weingard, being a top hand, soon got a job as ranch foreman near Mosquito Creek, where he remained for the rest of his life. Stillwell had enough of the whole thing and drifted back to Montana. Charlie rode on toward the Bloods' camping ground.

Indians had an intuitive gift for understanding the underlying motives of those with whom they came in contact. They recognized Charlie Russell as a spiritual brother and took him into their lodges as one of them. He had no trouble being accepted, and was taken to the chief, Sleeping Thunder. The chief could speak and understand a bit of English; Charlie was fairly good with sign language, so they were able to converse.

"I would like to stay with your people; live in their tepees, learn their ways; become as an Indian."

The old chief looked at him with piercing eyes for a long moment, then said, "Your heart is good. You speak with the straight tongue. You are welcome to stay as long as you wish."

Medicine Whip, an old warrior, was in the chief's lodge at the time.

"I would like our white brother to make my lodge his own," he invited.

Charlie rose to go with Medicine Whip, but Sleeping Thunder stopped him by asking, "What means your name, Charlie?"

Charlie shrugged. "I dunno. Nothin' I guess."

"What means Russell?"

"Nothin' that I know of. It's just my name."

"Your name among us will be Ah-Wah-Cous, meaning Antelope."

Charlie grinned, pleased. He knew instantly that the old chief referred to the buckskin reinforcement patch on the seat of his blue cowboy riding britches. Weingard had told him, also, that from the back he resembled a startled antelope, for these animals display in the rear a white flag of fluffed hair when they run. Charlie liked the name by which he would be called while he remained among the Bloods. He would often be called Ah-Wah-Cous by many of his white friends.

From the first he felt that he belonged among the Indians. He quickly learned their language and he was always welcome in the lodge of Sleeping Thunder when the old men and the warriors gathered for storytelling sessions, during which they recounted their brave deeds and unusual experiences. Charlie was able to absorb the lore of the Indians, their dress, their customs, their religion, how they thought and acted. He hunted with them and ate with them, even when he knew that the stew pot contained the flesh of a puppy—the Indians' favorite meat.

Painting occupied much of his spare time, and the Indians regarded his picture-making with awe, considering his ability to portray people and scenes magical. There was a beautiful Indian maiden whom he used time and again as a model. Her name was Kee-Oh-Mee.

"Why not marry Kee-Oh-Mee and stay with the Bloods?" Sleeping Thunder asked one day.

Charlie grinned in embarrassment. "I have no horses to leave at her father's tepee," he said by way of explanation. "I have but two horses, I can't part with either of them."

"You are a special one," Sleeping Thunder told him. "You do not need to buy your bride with horses and gifts because you use magic to make pictures. Kee-Oh-Mee looks upon you with favor. I can tell by the light in her eyes when you make her likeness with your magic brush."

"Kee-Oh-Mee is beautiful. She can have any young warrior in the village." Charlie put an end to the conversation.

He had been doing a lot of thinking during the months he had been among the Bloods, and Kee-Oh-Mee figured in many of those deliberations. Certainly she would be a good companion by his fireside. The idea of continuing to live as an Indian appealed to him—nor did the idea of being a "squaw man" repel him, for he had come to have great regard for the Indians who called him "brother."

He realized, however, that this primitive way of life was nearly over, as it had ended in Montana. Civilization was crowding too close. Frequently the red-coated Canadian Mounted Police rode into camp to let the Bloods know that they were being watched. Charlie knew that his friends were doomed. Soon they would be herded onto reservations.

Kee-Oh-Mee had teased him about his short hair. "Are your relatives all dead," she had asked, "that you cut your hair in mourning?"

"My relatives are living. I don't mourn," he had replied.

"Then," she had laughed derisively, "you must be afraid that the enemy will lift your scalp."

So Charlie let his hair grow. By the time it reached his shoulders he was able to endure doing without salt and sugar—the two items of diet he most missed. But he knew that he could never completely become an Indian. He was a poor hunter and could never become a warrior.

Having run out of paper and canvas, he tried painting on hides that Kee-Oh-Mee had tanned to soft whiteness for him. His paint brushes had finally worn out and he was reduced to using the chewed ends of twigs. His paints were getting low, as the scarcity of supplies handicapped him in his work more and more, he grew miserable.

But he finally had worked out the answer to the problem which he had come North to solve. He would not accept his wealthy would-be patron's offer to go to Philadelphia to study art. Paint he must, but he would do it his own way—not the way someone told him to do. He realized that he could not endure the crowded centers of civilization. He must remain in the uncluttered West he loved.

After making his decision, he felt as if a great weight had been lifted from his spirit. "Ah-Wah-Cous," he told himself, "the time has come for you to drift."

12

With the freighters

The six months that Charlie spent with the Indians in Canada did much to strengthen his philosophy of life. During that time he found himself as a person; he knew what he wanted to do.

Slowly he came to realize what direction his life should take. He knew that there was no future in cowboying, even though he loved the life. He had hoped to make his home in Judith Basin, but that entire part of the country was getting altogether too "civilized" to suit him. Perhaps summer jobs with the cow outfits would provide enough money to buy supplies. And perhaps his art work would eventually pay sufficiently to support him. Beyond this point his thoughts did not go. He was content to let each day take care of itself.

It was early March when he was seized with the impulse to return to Judith Basin. He chose about the worst time of the year in Montana to travel, for he planned to live on the land as he went, as an Indian would do. Once again he donned his cowboy garb with the white patch on the seat of his britches. His clothes were not warm enough for this time of year, but he would get along, he reckoned.

He was fortunate in coming across a train of overland freight wagons traveling south to St. Louis with a load of furs. The wagon boss was willing to have a strapping young cowboy accompany them through the Indian country, and it was certainly to Charlie's advantage to have three meals a day and be able to sleep in a covered wagon on bales of furs.

Charlie welcomed this opportunity to observe the workings of one of the colorful and exciting aspects of frontier life. The freighters were as picturesque as the cowboys and Charlie later used his firsthand knowledge to do several canvases depicting the freighter trains.

Three wagons were chained together and pulled by fourteen horses or oxen. The wagon boss was like the captain of a ship; his word was law. The jerk-line man was responsible for handling the animals that pulled the wagons. The driver rode the left horse and guided them by means of a single jerk line fastened to the bit of each animal. Sometimes, when going downhill, he rode on the seat of the wagon to be able to control the brake. Alongside each string rode the bullwhacker who urged the animals along by means of his long bull whip, which he was expert in handling. He could make it crack like a pistol shot or pick off a fly on the ear of the farthest ox.

The tons of freight aboard these trains made them coveted prizes of the renegade Indians who prowled the rough country through which the freight trains traveled, but there were no redskin attacks during the time Charlie traveled with the wagons.

He had no skill with a bull whip, but he had a strong voice, so while he traveled with the outfit it was his duty to ride alongside the teams and encourage them onward with shouts and cries. He stayed with the freighters until they were past the wide expanse of Northern Montana, then he bade his new friends good-bye and set out for Judith Basin at a fast pace.

First he went to visit Jake Hoover, where he did quite a bit of painting. From memory, he painted scenes from the Indian camp, from the Northwest Mounted Police, from the freight train. Although he finally could no longer put off a trip to Helena to replenish his supplies, he didn't have a dollar in his pocket. So when spring turned the grass green again, he rode off to Judith Basin to join the big spring roundup—the last such roundup in which he took part.

It made Charlie's heart sick to see the changes that had occurred: the cattlemen had welcomed the railroad, for it furnished a convenient way to market their cattle. But the railroad had also brought the homesteaders who came with papers that allowed them to fence off as much as one hundred and sixty acres of land. Naturally the newcomers looked for the land that contained water, so the range was no longer open to the great herds of cattle. Although the cattlemen had never held valid titles to any of the land, they considered it theirs by right of being there first. Charlie understood the bitterness of his cattlemen friends, for he knew that the land was not suitable for farming and that one hundred and sixty acres of rangeland would not provide a living for a settler family. But there was nothing that he or anyone else could do about the matter but accept the situation.

Sheepmen had also moved into the country, and the cattlemen detested sheep even more than they did fences. They claimed that the sheep ate the grass down to the roots and that their sharp hoofs destroyed it. A bitter resentment grew up between the cattlemen and the settlers. In some places, Wyoming, for instance, this enmity would flare into open warfare and bloodshed.

"We're worse than the Injuns," Charlie said plaintively to Jake. "The white men came along and killed off the buffalo, then shoved the redmen onto some dinky reservation. Now the nesters have come and spoiled the country for the cattlemen. I reckon the Bloods up in Canada have the right idea about living, but even they have the British Mounties nosing around all the time. Anyway, their way of living is still the best."

The cattlemen were moving their herds north to the Milk River country and Charlie went with them, taking up his old job as nighthawker. He also took a job for a brief time as guide to an English lord who came West to go on a hunt. Charlie made camp the first night and cooked the meal, then dished up the food and handed a tin plate to his employer. After heaping a plateful for himself and sitting down to eat, Charlie heard the nobleman sputtering, but he was too hungry to pay much attention.

"Listen my man," the Englishman finally said, "I'm

not in the habit of eating with my servants, don't you know."

"Zat so," Charlie mumbled with his mouth full. "Why don't you just wait till I'm through then, my good fellow."

Needless to say, Charlie took no more jobs as guide to titled Englishmen.

After getting a new supply of art materials, he spent more and more time painting. He sent several black and white sketches to Eastern magazines, most of which were rejected—but Charlie stubbornly kept on sending them. He had been much encouraged by the flattering comments that had appeared in the newspapers about his paintings. Although it was clear that there might be a possibility of making a living with his brushes, he had no idea how to start such a project except to go on drawing and sending out his efforts in hopes of attracting the attention of editors.

Frank Leslie's Illustrated Newspaper for May 18, 1889, reproduced a full-page drawing entitled "Ranch Life in the North-West—Bronco Ponies and Their Uses—How They Are Trained and Broken."

Meanwhile, on one of his trips to Helena, Charlie had met a man who proved to be instrumental in changing his life: Ben R. Roberts, a saddlemaker. From the first the two men had taken an instant liking to each other. It was Roberts who bought the original water color of "Waiting for the Chinook" from the owner.

Roberts knew of his friend's chronic state of being

short of money. "You ought to make a book out of your paintings," he suggested.

"Yeh? Well, for your information, that sort of project costs money. That's something that I don't have any of right now."

"Tell you what I'll do," Roberts went on. "You furnish the art work, I'll furnish the cash—attend to all the details. Then we'll split the proceeds."

Charlie chuckled. "I like your optimistic nature. You take it for granted there'll be proceeds to split."

"I'm sure of it—and I'm serious about my offer. You get on Monte and high-tail it over to Jake Hoover's cabin and do a dozen of your best paintings all the same size. While you're doing that I'll get busy and make the other arrangements."

"You're a gambler if I ever saw one," Charlie said. "But you've just bought yourself a proposition. I'll get a supply of canvas and paints and go to Jake's and get busy."

The result of Ben Roberts' generous offer was the publication in 1890 of an attractive tie-bound portfolio called *Studies of Western Life,* consisting of colored pictures of cowboys and Indians in characteristic actions. Granville Stuart, a prominent cattleman in Montana Territory, wrote the text. It was printed by the Albertype Company of New York City and widely distributed.

How much Ben Roberts and Charlie made on this joint venture has never been told. Probably Russell never bothered to total his earnings; Roberts merely told curious friends that he made a "nice profit." At any rate, the portfolio helped Charlie's growing reputation as an artist.

As a result of it he was commissioned to do an oil painting on the vault door of the bank at the booming town of Lewistown, Montana, not far from Judith Basin. It was an impressive piece of work and attracted considerable attention. In the foreground on a rocky cliff stood a handsome bronco with feet braced as though to protect himself from going over the edge. Seated on the horse with right leg hooked around the saddle horn, was a cowboy smoking a cigarette and gazing at the herd beyond. Attached to the cowboy and horse were the usual gear: chaps, revolver, cartridge belt, spurs and "ten-gallon" hat.

Charlie started working on the vault door at ten in the morning and finished about four in the afternoon. For this work he received twenty-five dollars—the largest sum he had earned yet with his brush—and at the moment it seemed to him a small fortune. Wrangling cows or horses for a whole month paid him not much more than he got for six hours' working. "No doubt about it," he told himself, "makin' a livin' as an artist ain't no bad idea!"

13

The struggle

In February of 1891 Charlie drifted to Lewistown. Cowboy jobs were scarce during the winter, but instead of "riding the line" he decided to stay in this town and see if he could eke out a living painting. When he ran into his good friend, Bob Stuart, the youngest son of cattleman Granville Stuart, the two of them decided to rent a shack and set up housekeeping.

Charlie began to work quite seriously and tried to find a market for some of his paintings. Most of them, however, went to pay grocery bills. When saloonkeepers were kind enough to put his art work on display, he sold quite a few for five or ten dollars apiece.

Russell had no knack for making money—nor was he able to keep the little he did make, for he had a soft heart and anyone with a hard luck story was able to walk away with a "loan." He was equally generous with his pictures: if somebody admired one, Charlie promptly gave it to him. Those who were willing to pay for his work he called "suckers."

One day he was amusing himself at a local hotel counter by modeling the figure of a bear from clay when a traveling man stopped to admire the miniature. "How much do you want for that?" he asked.

"Ten dollars," Charlie said jokingly.

"Oh, that's too much!" the man replied. "I'd be willing to give you five dollars for it."

Thereupon Charlie squeezed the figure in his hands and reduced it once more to a lump of clay. Dividing the clay into two parts, he quickly modeled a smaller bear from one of them.

"Here's your five-dollar bear," he said to the man.

A friend showed him an article that appeared in the April, 1891, issue of *Nature's Realm*. It was a direct result of his portfolio of Western paintings. In part it read:

> One of the best animal painters in the world is Charles M. Russell, of Montana, who is popularly known as the cowboy artist. His specialties are frontier scenes, wild Indian life, cattle pieces and natural history subjects, all of which are literal in their similitude and imbued with a truthfulness of character and detail . . .

"Whew!" Bob Stuart said after reading the article. "Who am I to bunk with an artist of such renown? You're too great for the likes of me."

"Bosh!" Charlie exclaimed. "I wonder who writes this kind of trash. How do these people even know my name?"

"You're becoming famous," Bob insisted.

Charlie snorted. "Fame doesn't butter any bread or

buy any beans. I didn't make much money wrangling cows, but I ate regular and good. That's more than I do as an artist. Next to cowboyin' I like paintin', but so far, my art work hasn't paid for many groceries."

"You'd eat a lot better if you didn't give most of your money away," his friend told him. "You're the softest touch I know. What you need is a manager."

"Want the job?"

Bob laughed. "Not I. I'm almost as soft a touch as you. I wouldn't know how to go about selling your pictures— But there must be a way. The papers and magazines are right: you're good. You've got to find a way to cash in on your talent."

Charlie hunched his shoulders. "I wish someone would come along and tell me how," he said wistfully. "Right now my bank account is definitely on the minus side."

Charlie did not realize it at the time but a whole school of literature had sprung up about the Indians, the pioneers, men like Kit Carson and Buffalo Bill. Now it was the cowboy who was riding in the saddle of popularity. Frederic Remington, the artist of western scenes, was already famous.

While Charlie was in Lewistown he received a letter from Charles Green, a bartender in Great Falls, offering him seventy-five dollars a month and board if he would do his painting in his bar. This proposition sounded good to Russell, so he saddled Monte, packed his few belongings on Gray Eagle, and with a cowboy friend, Frank Stough, set out for Great Falls.

They arrived in the busy, brawling cow town at night and made their way past noisy saloons, dance halls, and gambling houses to their hotel.

As they rode along the street Charlie drawled, "It's plain to be heard that this is a lively town."

Frank agreed that it would be a hard place to sleep except in the daytime.

The first thing the next morning Russell went to the Brunswick Bar and asked for Mr. Green. "Pretty Charlie," as he was called, turned out to be a genial man with a ruddy complexion and a waxed, pointed mustache. He advanced Charlie ten dollars, then drew out from beneath the counter a long contract. It stipulated that Charlie was to paint from six in the morning to six at night and that everything he drew, modeled, or painted for the next year was to belong to the bartender.

Charlie snorted. "There's some difference between painting and sawing wood."

He didn't care much for "Pretty Charlie" or his contract, so he handed back the money and walked out.

Going to another, more congenial place, Charlie soon became friends with several cowpunchers, a roundup cook and a prizefighter. All were, like himself, out of work. They decided to throw in and "batch" together. They rented a small shack on the south side of town. As Charlie later said of the adventure, "The feed was very short at times, but we wintered." Besides himself, the "Hungry Seven" consisted of Con Price, Bob Stuart, Al Mallison, Tony Crawford, Slim Trumbel, and John Crawford.

The shack in which this assorted group lived was called the "Red Onion," although no one remembers how it got the name. Since there were no bunks in the shack, the men merely spread their bedrolls on the dirt floor. They used apple boxes for chairs and had a small stove with a few pans and kettles. The place was crude and the comforts nil, but the company was good and Charlie was happy.

Such crowded living quarters were scarcely an ideal place for creative art work, but Charlie worked hard, for it was his paintings that furnished the livelihood for all seven.

One of the men with whom Charlie formed a firm friendship was Albert Trigg. As fast as Russell finished a picture, Trigg took it out and attempted to sell it. There were times that he sold a painting literally before the paint was dry. Although Charlie was painting under pressure, he was doing excellent work, and the same paintings that Trigg sold for five, ten, or fifteen dollars then are worth thousands of dollars today!

By spring Trigg seemed to have exhausted the market for Charlie's pictures and the Hungry Seven had to tighten their belts. One day Charlie heard that a wool buyer from Boston had expressed interest in his work, so Charlie picked up two paintings he had recently finished and this time he himself sought out the prospective customer.

"How much are your pictures?" the man asked.

"Fifty dollars," Charlie replied, squelching the impulse to duck his head between his hunched shoulders.

He was, of course, ready to lower the price. To his surprise the man drew out one hundred dollars and handed it to him.

Charlie gasped. He had meant fifty dollars for both pictures; the man obviously thought he meant fifty dollars apiece and seemed glad to get them at that price.

Charlie hurried to the grocery store and the Hungry Seven had full stomachs that night.

The Hungry Seven were high-spirited and good-natured and not above playing jokes on each other or anyone else who was handy. A pious lady of the town told Russell that she intended having the preacher in for a chicken dinner on a certain night. Charlie and his friends did not like the parson, so they helped themselves to three of the good woman's Rhode Island Reds, then threw the heads and feathers into the minister's back yard. Charlie met the lady in the grocery store and, managing to keep a straight face, asked her how the dinner was. She sputtered indignantly that someone had stolen the very chickens she had been fattening for the occasion.

Charlie widened his eyes. "I do declare," he said. "I was going past Preacher Jones' yard and saw some red feathers and rooster heads. But of course they couldn't be from your chickens."

"Henry," she told her son, "run over and take a look at those feathers."

The boy was back in a few minutes to report that the feathers did indeed look like those of her chickens.

"Well, he'll never be invited to dinner at my house again! No one else in town has Rhode Island Reds. I'm shocked that he could do such a thing."

Charlie had difficulty smothering his grin as he nodded his agreement.

14

Cupid throws a noose

ONE DAY CHARLIE RECEIVED NOTICE THAT HE HAD TO appear for jury duty. Never having been in court, he was rather disturbed by the summons and asked his friends what to do. After they told him many of the questions that he would be asked, he was a little uneasy. He was to appear the following day, but he didn't know at what hour.

Early the next morning while he was cooking breakfast, the phone rang and a voice asked, "Is this Charlie Russell?"

"It's nobody else."

The voice went on, "This is the courthouse. Don't you know you're called for jury duty?"

"Yes, but . . . ," Charlie stammered.

The voice said sternly, "No buts about it. Be here in ten minutes or you're subject to a fine and jail sentence."

It was about a mile to the courthouse and the streetcar was not running at that hour, so Charlie grabbed his hat and in his high-heeled boots started running. He had on his big red sash, and his hair was in his eyes. Everybody he passed stopped and stared at him.

He finally reached the courthouse, panting, and rushed into the courtroom, but there was no one but the janitor.

"Who you looking for? What do you want?"

As Charlie got his breath and looked around, it dawned upon him that he had been tricked. "I ain't lookin' for anybody, and I don't want nothin'. I've been jobbed," he said mornfully.

He had time to return to the shack and eat a hearty breakfast before time to show up for jury duty.

Every so often it became necessary for Charlie to feel the saddle under him and he usually rode to Cascade, about twenty-five miles from Lewistown. It exhilarated him to feel Monte's power beneath him, and to breathe in the fresh, clean air.

He had become fast friends with Ben Roberts, the "only man homelier than he was," Charlie said. The Roberts family were very fond of him, and he always received a warm welcome.

Charlie used the Roberts home as his mailing address and it was here that he received mail from his family. Mrs. Roberts and Mrs. Russell had struck up a correspondence and the goodhearted Mrs. Roberts kept Charlie's mother informed about her son's welfare and whereabouts.

Ben suggested that Charlie fix up the small lean-to shack behind the house for use as a studio and bedroom whenever he was in Cascade. While there he painted the three pictures that were reproduced in a large volume compiled by Charles Wallace entitled *The Cattle Queen of Montana.* That same year, 1893, he illustrated a book based on an old Indian legend, with text by John M. Beacom. This volume was later reprinted by a company that specialized in printing only the finest portfolios.

In February he found a letter from his mother waiting for him at the Robertses, asking him to come home for a visit. Although the communication did not say anything about her health, Charlie could read the urgency between the lines. He left for St. Louis in February and it was the last time he saw his beloved mother, for she died a few months later, after he had returned to Montana, this time to the small town of Chinook.

It was a golden fall day when he next rode to Cascade to visit his good friends. He went directly to Ben's saddle shop and, as usual, was invited to supper.

"Someday," Charlie said with his lopsided grin, "you're *not* going to invite me and I'll drop dead from shock."

"Well, don't drop dead yet," his friend advised. "There's a surprise in store for you."

"What is it?"

"I'm not going to tell you—it wouldn't be a surprise if I did."

That evening as Russell followed his friend into the kitchen he had forgotten all about the surprise. Suddenly, even before he greeted Mrs. Roberts or the children who had gathered about him, he stopped in his tracks, for there stood a young girl, as pretty as a wild rose.

"Charlie Russell," Mrs. Roberts said, "this is Nancy Cooper. Nancy, this is the cowboy-artist I've been telling you about."

As they nodded their heads to each other, Charlie was aware of a pair of sky-blue eyes looking him over and he felt his face turn hot. So this was the surprise! He should have been given some warning so that he wouldn't stand there gawking, fiddling with his hat, not knowing what to say or do. His heart was beating fast—never had he seen anything prettier than this girl.

Mrs. Roberts came to his rescue by asking, "Wouldn't you like to wash up? Dinner's almost ready."

Charlie dipped hot water into the washbasin and did an extra-good job of washing his hands and face.

Nancy must have looked him over with a very observing eye, for she later wrote an account of the meeting which was printed in Russell's *Good Medicine,* the volume of his letters published in 1929 by Doubleday:

> There was something different about this man. He took off his coat, a double-breasted blue serge, hung it on a chair back, turned very square shoulders and straight back to me and walked over to the wash bench. He was a little above average height and weight. His high-heeled riding boots covered small arched feet, his riding breeches of heavy blue army cloth were snug fitting. They were held up by a wonderful bright colored French half-breed sash that clung just above the hips. The sash was wound around twice, the ends twisted and turned into a queer

flat knot, the long fringe tucked into his hip pockets. He wore a gray flannel shirt unbuttoned at the throat with a necktie hanging loosely. . . .

His face, with its square jaw and chin, large mouth, tightly closed firm lips, straight nose, high cheek bones, grey deep-set eyes that seemed to see everything, was one with an expression of honesty and understanding, and a face I could not forget. In time I came to know that he could not see wrong in anybody. He never believed anyone did a bad act intentionally; it was always an accident.

His hands were good-sized, perfectly shaped with slender, long fingers. He loved jewelry and always wore three or four rings. They would not have been Charlie's hands any other way. . . . It was not the rings that attracted but the artistic, sensitive hands that had great strength and charm. When he talked he used them a lot to emphasize what he was saying much as an Indian would do.

While he washed I watched him as closely as possible without being observed. When he was drying his face there seemed to be a good chance to take a good look, from the boots up. By the time my eyes reached his head he was drying one side of his face and peeking out of the corner of the towel at me. He laughed and I almost dropped the plate of fried ham.

At the supper table in the soft light of the coal oil lamp he talked; we could see the play of laughing wrinkles on that Indian-like face. He looked like a blond Indian and had us fascinated with his stories of western life.

Nancy Cooper was sixteen, but mature for her age; Charlie was thirty when they met. That evening marked a change in both their lives.

When Mrs. Roberts went into the dining room, Charlie followed her. "Where did you find Nancy?" he asked.

"She's from Kentucky," the woman explained. "Her parents are separated and she's been having a difficult time. She was living in Helena with Mrs. Biggs when I coaxed her here to help me take care of the children. She's a wonderful person."

Mrs. Roberts gave him a keen look.

"Yes," he said and his eyes held a dazed look. "I can see that. She's mighty pretty too."

He was especially entertaining during dinner, and kept glancing over at Nancy to see how she was responding to his conversation; but for the most part she kept her blue eyes modestly downcast.

It was a clear-cut case of love at first sight with him. He remained in Cascade and began a serious courtship. In the evening they would take strolls along the bank of the Missouri and often stand on the bridge to watch the moonlight shimmering on the river.

Charlie was so much in love that one night he offered to give her Monte.

"Oh, I couldn't accept him," she told him. "Why, that would be like giving me your right arm."

"You can have that too," he told her. "Both arms and the man that goes with 'em. What I'm trying to say is that I love you. I'd like to make a pretty speech asking you to marry me, but I don't know how."

She smiled at him and there was mist in her eyes. "You made the prettiest proposal possible when you offered to give me Monte. Now I'm sure that you love me. I'll be proud to be your wife."

Charlie immediately went into a frenzy of painting. He was broke, as usual, and needed money to get married. He was lucky enough to sell three of his canvases, for which he received seventy-five dollars. He spent most of it fixing up Ben's little shack, where they would live. He painted the walls blue to match his Nancy's eyes.

They were married on September 9, 1896, in the Robertses' home, with only a handful of friends present. As Charlie later told one of his friends, "That night the preacher put me in double harness. Our weddin' trip was a hundred yards to that one-roomed shack—an' we walked."

The next day he sat down at the clean table and swiftly made two pen and ink sketches, both showing the interior of the little shack. One depicted the room shadowy with cobwebs, with skillets of beans and potatoes on the messy table where Charlie sat hunched over, eating. Dirty dishes were stacked about, clothing strewn over the floor. The companion picture showed the little place neat and shining, with a table properly set and Charlie eating with a look of happiness on his face.

Another picture he drew at this time showed a winged cupid astride a horse with his lariat around a man he had pulled from his mount. These drawings were Charlie's wedding announcements.

15

A place of his own

NOW THAT HE HAD A PRETTY YOUNG WIFE TO SUPPORT, Charlie set to work in earnest, putting more time and effort into his paintings; but even when he was able to sell them at his top price of twenty-five dollars, it was impossible to make a decent living.

Charlie was thirty-two when he got married, and set in his ways. Eighteen-year-old Nancy, however, was determined to "ride herd" on him, induce him to give up his rowdy ways with the "boys." From the first, Charlie's friends resented her efforts to keep such a tight check rein on her husband. Fortunately, his amiable good nature kept the little household from becoming too turbulent, for Nancy's temper flared up easily. At such times Charlie quietly put on his hat and walked out. By the time he returned, the tempest was over, but there is no doubt that Nancy was determined, so far as possible, to bring about some changes.

The little cow town of Cascade was hardly a good market for Charlie's pictures, even at the ridiculously low prices at which he sold them; so after talking the matter over for some time, the Russells decided to make a move, and they chose Great Falls. They realized that living expenses would be greater, since they would no longer have the Robertses' shack.

"You don't charge enough for your paintings," Nancy told Charlie. "From now on you *must* get more money. You're on the way to becoming famous, you know."

He grinned and patted her shoulder. "With you to spur me on, I ought to get someplace someday—if we don't starve to death first. Of course, I could always go back to cowboyin'."

"You're through cowboying," she said, her pretty little chin firm. "You're an artist. Someday you'll be very well known and people will be glad to pay thousands of dollars for your paintings."

Later he would write in one of his stories his opinion of a woman's role in a man's life:

> It's the women that make the men of the world. I heard an educated feller say once, 'n' it's the truth, that a man's going to hell or heaven, if you look at the trail ahead of him you'll find a track the same shape as his, only smaller; it's a woman's track. She's always ahead, right or wrong, tollin' him on. In animals, the same as humans, the female leads. . . . If you ever run buffalo, you notice the cow meat's in the lead. With wild horses, the stallion goes herdin' 'em along, from the looks you'd call him chief, but the mares lead to the water hole they've picked out.

One of Charlie's good friends, Charles Schatzlein, who had a hardware store in Butte, always exhibited Russell pictures in his window and he was able to sell some of them, the top price being twenty-five dollars.

Nancy told him, "Charlie's getting to be famous now. He must get more money for them. From now on, no picture of his will be sold for under seventy-five dollars. Look at Frederic Remington—he makes a fortune with his paintings."

Charles agreed with Nancy that Charlie was not getting enough for his paintings, and agreed to ask more for those he sold.

Charlie was still trying to sell drawings to the Eastern magazines, Remington's main outlet, but the results were discouraging, perhaps because the letters he wrote were full of misspelled words and grammatical errors.

Soon after they moved to Great Falls, Charlie received an offer from the small outdoor magazine *Western Field and Stream,* with a contract ready for him to sign. It read:

> Agreement between Charles Marion Russell, of Great Falls, Montana, and William Bleasdell Cameron, of St. Paul, Minnesota, made 30th of September, 1897.
>
> The said C. M. Russell agrees to make for the said W. B. Cameron twenty black and white oil paintings, about 24 x 18 inches in size, and twenty-one sketches about 12 x 18 inches each, comprising a pictorial history of western life, the whole to be completed within a reasonable time, or by the first of January 1898, if possible.
>
> The said W. B. Cameron agrees to pay said C. M. Rus-

sell the sum of fifteen dollars for each painting upon delivery of the twenty pen sketches.

It is further agreed between the parties that the paintings are to be reproduced and advertised from month to month in the *Western Field and Stream,* published in St. Paul, Minn., and they are also to be published in two books, upon completion, the paintings in one and the sketches in another, such books to be placed for sale upon the market and that said C. M. Russell shall have one-third interest in the copyrights of said books and all profits which may arise from the sale as aforesaid.

Witness: *Nancy Russell*

Signed: *C. M. Russell*
Signed: *W. B. Cameron*

Charlie had never signed a contract before, and Nancy was not very happy about Charlie's selling his paintings for such a small sum. But she agreed with him that this might open doors to other, more lucrative assignments and would certainly be good advertising.

Several articles appeared in the magazine under the by-line of William Bleasdell Cameron. Judging from the subject matter, the material for the articles no doubt came from Charlie, but at that time his style was not considered worthy of even a small magazine.

Before the contract was completed, the magazine was unable to continue payment, so not all the pictures were published and there is no record that the books were either.

The cupboard was very bare in their sparsely furnished home when Nancy first set out with one of Charlie's pictures to try to sell it herself. She had heard of someone who was interested in owning a Russell picture, and she lost no time in calling on him. When she reached her destination, she immediately unrolled the canvas, placed it in a favorable light, and then went on to explain the fine points of the picture. The man squinted at it and looked at it from all angles and finally asked the fatal words: "How much?"

"Seventy-five dollars," Nancy said in a determined tone, without a word of protest the man wrote a check for the amount.

On her way home Nancy stopped at the grocery store and that night the Russells had full stomachs. From that time on, Nancy did all of the selling of her husband's pictures. She gradually raised the prices and proved to be a very shrewd business woman.

Charlie was more than willing to have her take charge of financial matters, knowing full well that he was not able to manage them himself. As he said to Ben Roberts, "The lady I trotted in double harness with was the best booster and pardner a man ever had. She could convince anybody that I was the greatest artist in the world, an' that makes a feller work harder. You jest can't disappoint a person like that, so I done my best work for her . . . We're pardners, an' if she hadn't prodded me, I wouldn't have done the work I did. An' if it hadn't been for her, I wouldn't have a roof over my head."

The going wasn't easy, for people in and around Great Falls were too accustomed to seeing Charlie's pictures given away or used to pay grocery bills to really value them according to their worth. It was the strangers who came to town who bought the paintings at higher prices.

Charlie's father came West to visit and to get acquainted with his new daughter-in-law of whom he approved wholeheartedly.

"I'm proud of you, son," he said, slapping Charlie on the shoulder, "for bringing such a fine little woman into the family. I'm hoping that she'll get you to settle down now. I'm glad to see that you've given up being a cowboy and are concentrating on being an artist. You certainly have plenty of talent. I know it's hard to make a living as an artist, especially the first few years. I'll be glad to help you any time you need money."

Charlie grinned. "I've always needed money," he answered. "Always will, I reckon. Can't seem to hang on to it when I am lucky enough to get hold of some. But you know me: I'm independent. I always want to make my own way—always did. It's been rough on Mame [as he called Nancy], but she's as game as they come. If I ever amount to anything, it will be all her doing. She gets more for my pictures now than I ever expected to make."

His father looked around the poorly-furnished living room. "You need a better house . . ."

Charlie nodded. "That we'll have before long. We intend to use the legacy I got from Mom to build us a nice new home."

"Fine! Fine!" Mr. Russell said.

His father's visit gave Charlie great happiness and satisfaction. Never had he felt so close to the older man and he regretted that he had often worried his parents.

The lot where the young Russells chose to build their home was next door to Albert Trigg, Charlie's good friend. The new house was a comfortable, two-story white frame building, with good north light in the living room so that Charlie could use it as a studio.

In time, however, he began to yearn for a place that was entirely his own—a place where he could display the unusual and interesting Indian objects he had been collecting for years; a place where he could make a "muss" if he felt like it and Nancy wouldn't object; a place where his friends would feel free to drop in and where he could cook up a mess of grub.

There was plenty of room for such a studio next to their house, and with great enthusiasm Charlie began to make plans. There was a scarcity of logs, which he had wanted to use, so he decided to use telephone poles. At one end of the large room he would have a huge fireplace with a Dutch oven to use for cooking cowboy food for his friends. Across the entire front of the building there would be a low porch, the roof of which he planned to cover with elk horns.

After turning his plans over to a contractor, for some unaccountable reason he got the idea that the neighbors might object to having a log cabin so near by, and while the studio was being built he scarcely went near it.

One afternoon Albert Trigg came over for a visit. Finally he said, "Say, how about letting me see the inside of your studio? With that fine fireplace-chimney, it's a fine-looking place outside. It's an asset to the neighborhood, but I'd sure like to see it indoors."

Trigg heartily approved of the spacious interior. "I'd like to have something like this," he said. "A man needs a place where the womenfolk aren't forever cleaning up."

"I sure need it." Charlie grinned. "Naturally my painting makes considerable clutter. And of course I never could live up to Nancy's ideas of neatness. Wait until I get my Indian trophies on the walls. This will be a good place for us fellers to get together for cowboy grub and some good yarn-spinning, like us rawhides used to indulge in."

He fixed the studio to his liking and after working in it for a while it became his favorite spot—a room in which he felt entirely himself. And it was there that he did his best work.

16

The plan to "crash" the big town

Although Nancy steadily bombarded Eastern magazines with letters calculated to arouse their editors' interest in her husband's painting and sketches, for the most part the editors remained unresponsive. In 1899, however, eight Russell illustrations appeared in a small, privately printed volume of poems entitled *Rhymes of a Round-Up Camp,* by Wallace D. Coburn, but Charlie's name did not appear on the title page. A short time later a portfolio of twelve plates was published, very handsomely bound in limp black leather with gold letters, *Pen Sketches by Charles M. Russell, the Cowboy Artist.* Charles Schatzlein, Charlie's longtime friend who had always taken an active part in promoting Russell pictures, took over the distribution of this little volume. He was the president of the W. T. Rigeley Publishing Company, which brought out the portfolio. It did well locally, but its appeal was mainly for people who were interested in the cattle business. Its sale was not as widespread as Charlie and his friend had hoped, but it was a start and *Pen Sketches* was reprinted three times within the year.

One morning Nancy said to her husband, "There ought to be some way of reproducing those little figures you make just for the fun of it. They're excellent—sometimes I think you're as good as a sculptor as an artist. Maybe better."

He gave her one of his quizzical glances. "Just so you think I'm good for something."

"You're very good indeed," she told him emphatically. "And it makes me furious that by this time the world hasn't recognized what a fine artist you are."

He chucked her under the chin. "Having a pretty wife on the sidelines rootin' for me makes me work that much harder," he said. "Whether or not the world appreciates me, I know that I've done my best work since I married you. Your idea about makin' some sort of reproduction of my modeled figures might be a good one. I love to do 'em. I s'pose they'd have to be cast in bronze—an' that would cost money. Right now we're havin' trouble keepin' the grocery bill paid without any extra expenses."

"Why don't we take a trip to St. Louis to visit your relatives? At the same time we'll try to drum up some interest in your paintings and find out about getting your figures cast in bronze."

Charlie chuckled. "If you keep poppin' that old bull whip over my head, maybe I'll amount to somethin' yet, Mame. But you're right. We ought to go visit the relatives and let them see what a pretty little slave driver lassoed me. That oughta make 'em proud of me if nothin' else does."

So they traveled to St. Louis. He and his father enjoyed presenting the pretty bride to the numerous aunts, uncles, and cousins who invited them to dinners and parties. It was a gay social whirl and here Nancy saw her husband in a role she had only glimpsed before. As a storyteller he was unsurpassed. Among people to whom his stories were new, he performed like a polished actor. His listeners hung on his words and their interest stimulated his powers.

"Why, Charlie Russell!" Nancy exclaimed when they were alone in their room the first night she saw him hold a roomful of people spellbound. "I have never heard you go on like that before."

Thinking she was chiding him, he hung his head and looked shamefaced. "Did I talk too much? I didn't mean for to embarrass you. I know I don't speak grammatical. And these folks talk pretty elegant."

"Embarrass me!" she cried. "Why, Charlie, I was so proud of you! Your stories are wonderful; they bring the Old West to life. You ought to write them down—just the way you tell them. Never mind the grammar. Lots of folks can talk or write grammatically, but it's a rare person who can tell stories the way you told them tonight. Why haven't I heard you talk like this before?"

He gave his lopsided grin. "Shucks! Most of my buddies have heard those stories lots of times. That's just cowboy talk—when we get around the fire for a session—

everyone tells what happened to him. All the things I told tonight really happened—not all to me but to people I know. I reckon the reason you haven't heard me talk like that before is because that's the way me and the fellers talk when there ain't no women around. Of course the women here are thrilled by stories of the West, but Western women think it's old stuff. You never were one to want me to have my men friends around. That's why my log cabin studio comes in handy."

Mist came quickly to her eyes and he saw that he had hurt her. He put his arm around her shoulder. "Not that I blame you, Mame," he said. "You're so little and delicate."

"I don't mind your friends," she said. "It just that they always want to take you away from your work. Furthermore, they don't like me."

"It isn't that," he told her. "They just think you ride herd on me pretty close. They kid me about it, but I don't mind. You're good for me, and I like having you take care of me the way you do."

From a social point of view the visit to St. Louis was a success, and Charlie was interviewed by the local newspapers and some of his pictures reproduced, but the visit did nothing to further his career. He sold not a painting, even though he had brought along several that he hoped people would buy.

As soon as the Russells got back to Great Falls, one of the newspaper sent a reporter to their house for an interview. It took place in his studio and the reporter wrote:

> Indian robes and finery were scattered about. . . . On the walls were pen and ink sketches, water colors and oil, all the products of his gifted fingers. . . . The first impression of him fitted his title accurately. He is a cowboy artist and looks the part. His manner was unaffectedly hospitable and courteous. . . . He walks with the gait of a cowboy . . . a man who has spent much time in the saddle. . . . One sees but little of the artist in that large, strong, big-jowled face. . . . Modest of his accomplishments, not prone to talk of his work, carefully, almost boyishly, covering up his love of art and longing to accomplish great works . . .

His friend Trigg came over and asked Charlie how he liked the big city.

"You can have it," Charlie said somewhat bitterly. "There's nothing in the East for me. Even among my relatives I feel like an outsider. And what do Easterners care about my pictures? Why, they wouldn't give thirty cents a dozen for them . . ."

Trigg broke in: "I judge you didn't make many sales then."

"Not a one. They don't savvy me back East. It's the Western people who understand and want my pictures. Mame and I went to an exhibit that gave us an idea to see what those people like. They're all daffy about the new Impressionist School, they call it, from France. Craziest stuff I ever saw."

Trigg nodded in sympathy. He saw that his friend had been badly hurt, for he seldom criticized anyone or anything.

"In one gallery," Charlie went on indignantly, "we saw a landscape they were all raving about. Color! Why, say, if I ever saw colors like that in a landscape, I'd know I was loony. A man who would paint a thing like that and represent it as a copy of nature oughta have his head examined."

"That's what I like best about your pictures," Trigg said soothingly. "You represent nature just as it is. And everyone of your pictures tells a story. You're putting down permanent history of this part of the country in pictures."

Charlie grinned. "You make me feel better, Al. I've been pretty low in spirits ever since I got back."

"Did you find out anything about having your sculptured figures cast in bronze? You said you hoped to."

Charlie shook his head. "All I learned was that the work would have to be done in New York— And it's darned expensive, they tell me. So I reckon that finishes me as a sculptor."

In his log studio Charlie felt completely natural and did not have to worry about cluttering up Nancy's neat house. Here his old friends and new—cowboys, saloonkeepers, Indians, grub-line riders—all felt free to drop in and spin yarns. Whenever Charlie felt the urge, he cooked up cowboy meals in the big fireplace for his visitors. Altogether, it had been an inspiration to build a place of his own. Nancy was beginning to understand the facet of her husband's nature that required him to be with his friends or to seek solitude and allow the ideas for his pictures to form and grow.

Among the new friends Charlie made were Will Crawford and John Marchand, two fairly well-known illustrators who were traveling in the West. They had heard of the cowboy-artist and had made it a point to meet him. Both men were greatly impressed by his talent. "You must come to New York," Crawford insisted. "That's where you'll make the contacts that will help you find the success you deserve."

"Yes," Marchand agreed. "We'll be glad to introduce you to a few editors and publishers."

"I'd be lost in New York." Charlie scratched his head, frowning. "Why, I even feel that way in St. Louis where I grew up. It's the wide-open spaces for the likes of me. I sort of got the cold shoulder when I was in St. Louis not long ago. Easterners don't cotton to my art."

"It takes time to build up a reputation," Crawford said. "Believe me, you'll have to crash New York before you ever get into the big time. It won't be easy, but you'll just have to make up your mind to go there and have a showing. In time it will pay off."

"I'd rather have all my teeth pulled. Riding herd on stampeding longhorns would be a sight easier for me," Charlie responded.

Before they left, the two men told Nancy that she should try to persuade her husband to go to New York with a collection of his pictures. She agreed with them enthusiastically. "I'll see what I can do," she promised.

17

Success long overdue

IN SPITE OF NANCY'S INSISTENCE THAT THEY GO TO New York, Charlie kept holding back. It wasn't just his reluctance to plunge into the "Big Camp" as he called it; it was also their chronic shortage of money.

While they were still considering the pros and cons of the matter, a letter came from Charlie's father urging him to send some of his pictures to the Louisiana Purchase Exposition in St. Louis, opening May 1, 1904. Charlie was reluctant to offer anything, but Nancy convinced him that he should do it.

The St. Louis *Post-Dispatch* for December 6, 1903, carried a story about Charlie Russell in its Sunday magazine section, headlining it:

COWBOY ARTIST WHO HAS LIVED AMONG THE INDIANS FOR TWENTY-THREE YEARS WILL EXHIBIT STUDIES AT THE WORLD'S FAIR.

He sent three large paintings to the Fair; however, he reserved the choicest pictures for his New York trip.

Nancy had at last persuaded him that they should go. Dressed in their Sunday best, the Russells said good-bye to their friends and set out for the long train ride to New York, loaded down with paintings and drawings.

Charlie soon left Nancy, who had struck up a conversation with a woman across the aisle, and went to the smoking car. He was in the habit of making friends wherever he went, for his easygoing manner and good disposition usually attracted people to him. But the men in the smoker with whom he tried to chat looked at him as though they expected him to pick their pockets. He gave up trying after a few attempts and went back to join Nancy.

On the second day of the trip he went to the smoking car again and sat down next to a stranger but this time he did not try to make conversation.

"Howdy!" the stranger said.

Charlie turned to face a man who grinned at him in a friendly manner. He had dark hair, a straggly lock of which hung over one of his twinkling blue eyes. His manner was engaging and he was chewing gum with considerable vigor.

Charlie felt drawn to him immediately. "Howdy," he responded. "My name is Charlie Russell."

"Mine's Will Rogers. From Oklahoma."

"I'm from Montana. I'm on my way to New York to try to interest the big boys in some of my paintings."

"Why, I've heard of you!" Rogers exclaimed. "You're the cowboy-artist. I've seen your pictures in magazines."

"Too few magazines," Charlie said with his crooked grin. "That's why I'm goin' to New York. I don't believe that much will come of it, though."

"That's a coincidence—it sure is." Will Rogers also had a lopsided grin. In fact there was a slight resemblance between the two men. Perhaps it was in the way the unkempt hair of both hung over their eyes. "I'm trying to crash the big time too. I tell bum jokes, but people laugh for some reason or other. And I spin a lariat. Used to be a cowboy of sorts. That's all I wanted to be when I was a kid."

"Well, this is a coincidence, sure enough. I used to be a cowboy—that's all I wanted to be when I was a kid. Fact is, I'd still like to be one, or an Injun, if times was like they used to be."

Each man recognized in the other a kindred spirit and the journey to New York seemed much shorter to Charlie because of the worthwhile friend he had just made.

Reaching New York, they had to go their separate ways but continued to meet whenever they could for a "quick lunch." The warm friendship they formed then was to endure through the years.

As Will Rogers later wrote:

> Charlie Russell was trying to sell a few paintings and I was trying to sell a few jokes . . . We met going East. Neither of us had much more than carfare, and the free lunch counter had a strong appeal to both of us in those days. As a matter of necessity, we both had to patronize the cheap lodging houses. That was before either of us

was known much outside of his own home town. He went up the ladder of fame a lot faster than I did.

He is the only painter of Western pictures in the world that cowpunchers can't criticize. Every little piece of leather or rope is just where it should be. So, you see, in these times of scandal, it is a pleasure to point out to you someone who had gained fame and still remains PURE.

Charlie and Nancy took a room in an inexpensive hotel called the Park View, located only a block from the studio that John Marchand and Will Crawford shared. Charlie wistfully observed that there was no view of a park from their small hotel room. It was only the insistence of his two artist friends that kept him from taking the first train back West. They found an inexpensive basement room where he could exhibit his paintings; they also took him around and introduced him to editors, publishers, and such important men in art circles as Ernest Thompson Seton, the great naturalist-painter-writer.

Nancy had hoped that wealthy New Yorkers would visit the exhibit and buy her husband's pictures, and that editors and publishers would be impressed enough with his art work to give him assignments. But no one came except some of the people Charlie had met in the Crawford-Marchand studio.

Nancy arrived at the little showroom early in the morning and she waited until late in the evening for customers. Charlie hung around, rolling one cigarette after the other and giving everyone who spoke to him his lopsided grin. Everyone praised his work, but no one bought.

Among the pictures on display was a fine, large water-color entitled "Roping a Grizzly." Years later President Taft would purchase this picture to hang in the White House; not long ago it was sold in New York for thirty-five thousand dollars. But when it was first placed on sale no one made an offer for it.

Charlie was disheartened, but Nancy tried to cheer him up by saying that it took time to get started. After two weeks money was running short and they could no longer afford the basement studio. "I'm ready to call it quits. Let's go home," he said in disgust. "It makes me sick to think that we've spent all our money on a wild-goose chase."

"We're not leaving yet," Nancy told him firmly. "You set up your easel in John and Will's studio—you may learn something from them and their friends. At any rate, it will give you someone to visit with. Meanwhile I'll take some of your pictures around to publishers and see if I can't interest them."

"You're a great little soldier, Mame," he said. "If I took on that sort of thing I'd certainly flub it. I just wouldn't have the nerve to walk up to an editor and ask him to buy my stuff. Ernest Thompson Seton says that's the way he got his start, but I'm just not made like that."

"I know you're not. In some ways you're just a big, shy, clumsy boy. You tend to the painting; I'll tend to the selling. Someday people will come begging to buy your pictures—they'll be willing to pay amounts up in five figures for them."

He chuckled. "What wild dreams you have, my darling. I wish I felt as optimistic! Right now I just hope you'll manage to sell enough so that we won't have to walk home. It's a long way."

Nancy hauled rolls of his canvases around from office to office and did manage to sell a few pictures. She also got several assignments for him, but their "crashing" of New York was far from a financial success.

Thus far Charlie had modeled his small wax or clay figures mainly for his own or his friends' amusement. While he was sharing the Crawford-Marchand studio he fashioned a clay figure of a drunken cowboy on a bucking bronco. The man's mouth was open; he held his six-shooter high in the air. Charlie called the figure "Smoking Up." Everyone who saw the small statue admired it.

John Marchand said, "You ought to have that figure cast in bronze."

"There's nothing I'd like better," Charlie drawled. "But what do you suggest I use for money?"

Will Crawford put in, "I hear that you can sell reproduction rights for a lump sum. Let me see if I can make the arrangements."

As a result of his friend's efforts, Charlie received one hundred dollars for the rights, and six bronze castings were made.

Meanwhile Nancy had interested *Leslie's Weekly* enough to have them print a story about her husband which appeared on March 3, 1904, along with reproductions of some of his pictures. The same publication also used his "Navajo Indian Horse Thieves" for their cover on April 21. *Outing Magazine* also used a story about Russell with three of his pictures in its December issue.

"We've got our foot in the door!" Nancy gloated.

Charlie grinned at her. "Thanks to you, we have money enough for the fare home—if we eat light. I was scared to death we were going to have to borrow."

Charlie was overjoyed to be back in Montana again, as an interview in the February 16, 1904, Great Falls *Daily Tribune,* proves:

> Charlie Russell, "the cowboy-artist" and Mrs. Russell returned yesterday from a visit of four months in the East, and incidentally it may be said that Charlie Russell is the happiest man in Great Falls.
>
> Russell's appearance on the streets yesterday was a glad sight to his scores of friends and he was kept busy shaking hands and saying "Howdy" to the many who pressed around him to welcome him back. . . . He is the same old "Charlie" and his comments on the East kept his auditors in a roar of merriment.
>
> "New York is all right, but not for me," he said. "It's too big and there are too many tall tepees. I'd rather live in a place where I know somebody and where everybody is somebody. Here everybody is somebody, but down there you've got to be a millionaire to be anybody.
>
> "The minute you get west of Chicago you can notice the difference in people. You begin to strike Westerners again. If you go into a smoking car east of Chicago, sit down beside a man and start talking to him by saying, 'This is a fine country around here,' he'll mumble, 'Yes,' and look the other way. You can't get anything out of 'em.

I guess they're afraid you'll spring a shell game on 'em or try to sell 'em a gold brick."

Although the trip was a financial disappointment, enough assignments dribbled in as a result of that first visit to convince Charlie that they should go East once a year. On their second trip Charlie detested the "Big Camp" as much as ever. He had never been so lonely as he was when he went out on the street and was surrounded by throngs of people who did not know him or "care a hoot" about him.

He sent a finely illustrated letter to Albert Trigg:

> . . . as I am lonsum tonight an far from my range I thaught it might help to write you just think I am in a camp of four millions an I guess I know about eight it makes me feel small . . . the whits are shure plentyfull. . . . I havent heard from there since I left only through Nancy an that don't tell me much of the bunch I mix with . . .

This trip proved to be much more profitable than the first one. Charlie again shared the studio with Crawford and Marchand, and while there he sculptured three of the finest miniature groups he had ever done. They were considered by critics the best specimens of their kind ever produced by anyone. They were "Blackfoot War Dance," "Counting Coup," and "The Buffalo Hunt," and were cast by the Roman Bronze Works.

Before returning to Montana, Charlie and Nancy had the satisfaction of seeing reproductions of the three groups displayed in the window of Tiffany's. The Russells got up nerve enough to step inside the fashionable store and inquire the prices of the figures. When they were told that the smallest one was one hundred and eighty dollars and the two largest ones were four hundred and fifty dollars apiece, Charlie whistled in surprise.

"Whoever would pay such outlandish prices?" he asked.

"Oh, we will sell them in time," the clerk told him.

"I hope so!" Charlie exclaimed.

The clerk looked surprised by this remark and Nancy said proudly, "My husband is the sculptor of those figures. He will get a royalty on each one sold."

Nancy's efforts also proved to be more fruitful than they had been the previous year. Charlie was commissioned to write a series of his own stories for *Outing Magazine* which were later published in book form as *Rawhide Rawlins Stories.* He was also given assignments to illustrate Stewart Edward White's "Arizona Nights," for *McClure's Magazine*; B. M. Bower's book, *Chip of the Flying U*; and W. T. Hamilton's *My Sixty Years on the Plains.*

Nancy was jubilant. "What did I tell you?" she cried. "You are well on your way to fame!"

"With you to prod me on," he replied, "I might make the grade. If it's necessary to make this trek once a year, I guess I can stand it—but I'll sure be glad to get back to Great Falls and my own log-cabin studio."

In 1905 the local newspaper reported his comments after he returned:

"Lordy, but this is good! Were you ever in a close room an' had to stay until the meeting was over, and finally you got so that you felt that you'd have to get out in the open or bust? Well, that's me. I'm right from New York, an' I want to say that New York's all right for them who like that sort of rush an' crush an' pack an' jam; but for me, I want room, I want breathing space, I want land big enough to turn around in without jostlin' anybody, an' I've come back to Montana to get it.

"One of my friends back there told me he wanted me to see the Catskill Mountains. I saw them, an' I couldn't help laughin'. An' when I got back to Billings an' got out on the platform an' breathed in all the Montana Ozone my lungs would hold, an' saw ever'where about me the towerin' peaks that have been part of my life for so many years, I felt a sort of pity for people back East who have to content themselves with potato hills masqueradin' under the name of mountains. . . .

"The cliff dwellers live high in New York, but they didn't have me skinned much. I was camped over timber-line myself. I'll take Great Falls Main Street, bumps an' all, instead of Broadway. New York with cars under ground an' sky-sailin' car lines is all right for them that likes her, but I likes this town with its two miles of track an' a few hacks. It's swift enough for me. Give me a camp where I savvy people."

18

Success!

CHARLIE'S GOOD FRIEND, CON PRICE, HAD FILED ON A homestead at the head of Kicking Horse Creek a few miles south of the Canadian border. Besides the three-hundred-and-sixty-acre homestead, Con's ranch consisted of three thousand acres of fenced government grazing land. However, he did not have money to stock the ranch.

One day Charlie went to the ranch to visit and he soon sensed his friend's trouble. "Tell you what I'll do," he offered. "I've been hankering to get myself a little spread where I can go whenever the notion takes hold to get away from civilization. Someplace where I can sketch and ride and feel a good horse under me. I'll file on the adjoining homestead and pay for stocking the ranch. You figure out the deal and we'll be partners."

There was no signing of papers. Each man trusted the other to be as honest as he was.

Con stocked the ranch with three hundred head of cattle and sixty horses. The cattle brand was the

Lazy KY. Charlie was not interested in the cattle business; he liked the little ranch because he could be out-of-doors and feel free. Here he turned his old friend Monte to pasture until the pony died of old age. In 1911 they sold the Lazy KY. Con appeared in Great Falls one day carrying the account books.

"What've you got there?" Charlie demanded.

"I brought these accounts so you could go over the ranch figures."

"Nonsense!" Charlie responded. "Burn 'em up and give me your check. Your word's good enough for me."

Charlie missed the ranch, but he kept a saddle horse in town and managed to ride nearly every day. Every spring the wanderlust seized him and he had to take his bedroll and camping equipment and head for the Judith Basin wilderness country, where he would stay for several days.

Every summer he visited the Piegan Indians on their reservation during their festival. He slept in a tepee and for the two or three days he was in camp he ate with them and lived like an Indian, although he did not join their ceremonies. He had not forgotten the sign language and his fingers flew as he conversed with the men.

The Indians loved him and looked forward to his visits. He always left camp loaded down with war bonnets, beaded moccasins, Indian dresses, and other souvenirs which he used to adorn his studio.

One of his favorite camping spots was on the shore of the lovely Lake McDonald. He grew to love the place more and more and finally built himself a comfortable log cabin to serve as his wilderness studio. He always got up early when he and Nancy stayed there, and made his own breakfast, allowing his wife to sleep. Then he'd take a long walk with a sketch pad under his arm. Much as he loved people, a part of him still demanded solitude.

He fashioned gnomes and pixies out of wood or clay and set them in nooks beside the path and the brook. He named his little retreat Bull Head Lodge after the buffalo skull he used with his signature on all his paintings. He allowed no hunting on his property; the birds and animals were unmolested and seemed to sense that they were safe around the cabin and became quite tame.

There was a beaver colony nearby and Charlie delighted in watching these shy creatures hard at work early in the morning. In the quiet forest he was able to study the many faces of nature.

By now Brown and Bigelow, the largest calendar manufacturer in the world, had begun to use his paintings on large calendars and these pictures soon became collector's items. Not only was he paid well for the original art work; it was always returned to him to sell. The calendars were a profitable source of income and, since they were widely distributed, they served as excellent advertisement for Russell's art.

He and Nancy kept knocking at the doorway of success through New York. They returned there every year and each visit was more profitable than the last. But it was not until 1911 that he won the recognition that was so long overdue. He was invited to have a one-man show at the

Folsom Galleries, where his pictures were grouped under the title, "The West That Has Passed." From now on Nancy would not have to visit publishers' offices with Charlie's canvases under her arm; henceforth people would come to him.

The New York *Times* as well as the *World* ran full-page stories with illustrations about him and his work in their Sunday editions. The *Times* wrote:

> "Cowboy" Russell . . . has come from Montana for his first "one-man exhibition." He has brought with him a score of paintings and bronze groups of Indians and cowboys and wolves and buffaloes that are making him famous. . . . His exhibition will be held in the Folsom Galleries . . . He will array there his "Medicine Man." . . . His "Disputed Trail" and "The Wagon Boss" and . . . "A Bunch of Indians Just Looking for Trouble"—lonely trails wolves—gun play . . . bony, wise-looking horses—gaudy trappings and blankets and feathers—buffaloes—that is all you will see at the Russell exhibition. . . . The trips he makes to the East only make him keener to get back to his West. "Me stay in the city? . . . If I had my way I'd put steam out of business!" In those rough words, rapped out beneath scowling brows, Russell, Westerner of the past, throws down the gauntlet to the present. "Gee, I'm glad I wasn't born a day later than I was!"—That's how Russell talks when he's interviewed. "It's mighty hard to know what to say," he grunts, taking off his cowboy hat, scratching his head and looking uneasily at the questioner's pencil. . . .
>
> "Oh, I have always made a bluff at painting," he explains when pressed for information about the beginning

of his career . . . He has also been modeling all his life. . . . He saw the taming of the wild cow towns . . . the whistling of the last bullets that flew in bloody brawls. Ever since he has been driven by an unquenchable thirst to portray the West before it vanished forever.

The Russells had not been back in Great Falls very long following Charlie's successful one-man show when he received a letter from the Honorable E. L. Norris, Montana's governor. Nancy brought it to Charlie's studio, and he tore the envelope open with nervous hands. He read the letter slowly, then reread it before handing it to Nancy saying, "Here, read this out loud. I don't think I got it right."

"It's an invitation, or summons, or command," she said, her voice quivering, "whatever you want to call it, for you to appear before the State Board of Examiners regarding the painting of a large historical canvas for the wall of the new wing of the State Capitol Building."

Charlie scratched his head and said, "Are you sure that's what it says? Maybe someone is jobbing me."

"This is no joke," she said. "It's signed by the governor. Charlie Russell, you have arrived. I always knew you would."

The result of the meeting was that Charlie was commissioned to do the big canvas for five thousand dollars. It was decided that the painting should show the historic meeting of Lewis and Clark with the Flathead Indians in Ross's Hole. Charlie journeyed to this spot many times while the painting was in progress to do sketching and to get the feel of the place. It took him about six months to finish the huge picture.

The painting of that historic meeting was the most ambitious canvas Russell had ever attempted. To be used as a mural on the wall behind the speaker's chair in the Montana House of Representatives, it formed a panel twenty-six feet long and twelve feet high.

The scene represented an early September sunset with the snow-capped peaks of a majestic mountain range as the backdrop. The meeting at Ross's Hole was a high point in the Westward trek of Lewis and Clark. They had traveled as far toward the sunset as the knowledge of their guide, Sacajawea, could take them. In the picture, the white men and a Negro, York, have crossed the stream and are standing close to the Indian camp. Lewis and Clark are in advance of their group; Sacajawea is seated on the ground. A Shoshone guide is conversing with the Flatheads in sign language, telling them that these men have brought them gifts from the Great White Father. The Indians advancing from their tepees in the background are mounted on ponies, dressed in fringed elkskin robes decorated with dyed porcupine-quill embroidery.

Every piece of Indian gear, as well as all the other items, was exact to the tiniest detail. Not only would this work be considered by critics as his best work; it would be regarded as the finest historical art work in existence.

The demand for Russell paintings increased, as did

the prices for them. Now that New York had been conquered and her husband's fame had spread from coast to coast, Nancy looked around for new worlds to conquer. Deciding that he should take a collection of his pictures to Europe to exhibit, she made arrangements for showing them at the famed Doré Galleries, which had shown exhibits of the best artists of the world.

They crossed the Atlantic on the *Oceanic* but did not enjoy the very rough sea voyage. It was early spring of 1914 when the Russells arrived in England. Among the twenty-five pictures that Charlie brought were several that remain favorites today: "When Sioux and Blackfeet Meet," "Wild Horse Hunters," "The Jerk Line," "The Queen's War Hounds," "The West That Has Passed."

After the pictures were hung a big banner was strung across Bond Street announcing in large letters:

CHARLES M. RUSSELL, COWBOY PAINTER OF THE WEST THAT HAS PASSED.

From the newspapers' rave notices of the showing and the record attendance crowds, it was clear that the English responded favorably to his art. Many titled persons visited the Russell exhibit; even the Queen Mother Alexandra with her sister, the Dowager Empress of Russia, were among those who attended.

Charlie himself was as much of an attraction as his pictures. Wearing his customary half-breed sash of red and his black boots, he was a figure to attract attention, and all who met him found him a colorful and distinctive personality.

The Russells were invited to attend numerous social functions. Charlie bowed to fashion to the extent of wearing a tuxedo when it was required; but he still wore his sash and cowboy boots (although he did wear his trouser legs outside instead of tucked into the footwear).

Later he told about one of the affairs he attended: "Sir Ramsey was pullin' off a reception to which Nancy an' I had been invited. I'd been handed our hostess for my pardner when we went into the dining room an' I'd sure been handed a bunch. She was so large that we couldn't both get through the door of the dinin' room at the same time; so I steps back an' stands on her train. Say, she packed and pulled on that dress like a cayuse on a rope. I gets off pronto, jes' as soon as I felt the strain. But I'm too late, an' she rips a lot of her gown. Then I simply straddles the long-tailed contraption an' we goes in tandem till there's room 'nough to get in double harness ag'in."

While in England, Charlie did only a few water colors, in addition to the illustrated letters he sent to friends back home. These were greatly treasured; no one ever threw away one of Charlie's letters, for they were all distinctive and always enlivened with water colors. Years later they were collected and published by Doubleday under the title *Good Medicine*.

Charlie and Nancy visited Paris with some friends, but Charlie was too homesick to travel to other countries. He had had enough of Europe. When he got off the train at Helena he drew in great gulps of fresh Montana air. "There ain't nothin' like this in England or Europe," he said. "I guess that air over there is awful old. Been breathed a lot or somethin'. It don't smell or feel as good in a fellow's lungs."

Late in his career he was commissioned to do a mural in the home of a very wealthy man in Helena. When the check for the painting arrived in the mail, he stared at it for a long moment, then handed it to his wife. The check was for thirty thousand dollars.

"Why, Mame!" he exclaimed. "That's dead man's prices! A few years ago I was glad to get ten dollars for a picture."

The days of struggle and poverty were over. Charlie was amazed at the high prices his pictures brought; sometimes he teasingly called Nancy a highway robber because she charged and got such outrageous sums. But he was grateful to her too, admitting that if it hadn't been for her, he would still be paying his grocery bill with paintings.

The fifteen years of hard work on his part and utmost determination on Nancy's paid off well. The Great Falls *Tribune* reported on January 15, 1915, that, back in Cascade in 1899 one of Russell's large paintings, "The Last Stand," had been raffled off to raise money for some charity. But the tickets, too high-priced, had not sold well. Just before the drawing, a banker, Frank P. Atkinson, had purchased all the remaining tickets for three hundred dollars. He won the picture and spent one hundred dollars more to frame it handsomely, then he hung it in the Cascade Bank. John J. Marony, President of the

First National Bank of Great Falls, who long coveted this particular painting, finally bought it for five thousand dollars and brought it back to Great Falls to be hung in his bank. Within fifteen years the canvas had brought its first buyer a handsome profit of forty-six hundred dollars. Atkinson remarked that purchasing Charles Russell pictures was like investing in a paying gold mine.

That same year, 1915, Russell paintings were shown in many major cities throughout the country. Now Charlie and Nancy had everything they wanted except the one thing they most desired: a child of their own. Charlie was extremely fond of children and they always flocked about him wherever he went. Every Christmas he fashioned clever miniatures for the house as he would have done for children of his own, and he heaped gifts upon his friends' children. At last the Russells adopted a baby boy whom they named Jack Cooper Russell and in a short time they loved this small bundle as if he were their own flesh and blood. Charlie's pride in the boy is shown in many of the letters he wrote:

> Friend Bill:
>
> . . . my wife got a letter from your best half asking us to come to camp with you all. We both thank you verry much but we wont worke your range this year. Wev got a six months old boy at our camp and we think hes a little young for trail work. . . . The stork didn't bring him. He had been on earth about three moons when he was thrown in my cut but hes wearing my Iron now and I hope nobody ever vents it.

Friend Con:

Maybe you dont know it Con but we got a boy at our house now. He was a little two months slick ear when we put our iron on him. Hes a yearling past now and wer shure stuck on him. His name is Jack . . .

Friend Tex:

. . . Several months ago I got a card from you saying you was a Dad of a son. Youv got nothing on us but ours wasnt waring our brand but his brands vented so hes ours all right and we sure love him. He's a yearling past now and it keeps us both riding heard on him . . .

Friend Con:

. . . I am sending you a couple of pictures of Jack . . . Hes shure a fine boy and loves horses. Hes got a rocking horse and two stick horses and he rides the tail off the hole string. I still have a cople of old cyuses and some times I take him in the saddle with me and it shure tickles him . . .

When Jack grew old enough to enjoy stories, Charlie told them by the hour. As Nancy watched and listened, she thought that the little boy was the best audience her husband ever had.

Jack was a golden-haired lad with a sunny disposition. His laughter and childish prattle brightened the white frame house. Charlie was like an overgrown puppy in playing with the little fellow. "He sure makes life worth living, doesn't he?" he often said to Nancy. "I feel twenty years younger and a million times happier since we got him."

Nancy agreed.

Charlie usually took the little boy with him on his daily walks. The proud father liked to show Jackie off.

Charlie, Nancy, and baby Jack began to take yearly trips to California to escape the harsh Montana winters and to display Russell pictures. Charlie, of course, looked up his old friend, Will Rogers, who by now had also become famous. Rogers introduced the Russells to other famous people such as Douglas Fairbanks, Sr., Fred Stone, Irvin S. Cobb, Annie Oakley, William S. Hart, and many others.

Since going to California each winter had become a habit with them, they decided to build a pueblo-style house on the edge of Pasadena—a home they were never to inhabit.

Charlie became afflicted with sciatic rheumatism and was in bed for months. For a long time afterward he had to use crutches.

He wrote to Will James:

> . . . I have been in bad shape for nearly a year but am better now. Tryed to get on a horse the other day at Harry Carey's ranch but couldent make it can't ride nothing wilder than a wheel chair . . .
>
> I appreciate your invite to come to your home and am glad you have a nice place and I will come sometime. This goes both ways. I have a camp in Glacier Park where the pipe is lighted and the robe is spread anytime you come . . .

But even after his sciatica left him, Charlie felt miserable. He went to Mayo Brothers' Clinic at Rochester,

Minnesota, where the doctors operated on him to remove a goiter. When it was all over he asked the doctors how he had fared.

"Tell me the truth," he said. "Even if the verdict isn't favorable, I want the facts."

They told him that he might live for not more than six months. His heart was in poor condition because he had waited so long for the operation.

"If that's the way it is, so be it," he said. "I didn't expect to live forever. But please don't tell Nancy."

Nancy, however, already knew. "Don't tell Charlie," she begged the doctors. "I want his last days to be as happy as possible."

So each went on until the end pretending to the other that all was well—that Charlie had a long, serene life before him. And each did all in his or her power to bring happiness to the other. Albert Trigg advised Nancy to give up the project of finishing the home they were building in Pasadena because of its great expense. She refused lest Charlie guess the truth about his condition. Trigg went to Charlie with the same suggestion, but Charlie also refused, for the same reason.

Never had Charlie and Nancy been so close and, in spite of the doom hanging over them, their last months together were serene and happy.

Although Charlie now had to avoid any sort of exercise, he could still paint, which he did, feverishly, in order to finish as many pictures as possible in the time he had left. And what a record it was. In spite of the reckless scattering about of his early work, there are known to exist twenty-five hundred of his paintings, seventy bronze figures, and literally hundreds of pen-and-ink drawings and illustrated letters. Numerous museums proudly display his art today.

He was working against time to get as much work done as possible; he was also devoting hours of every day to Jack, playing with him, seeking through stories to lay a firm foundation for good character.

Since he could no longer ride horseback, he, Nancy, and Jack went for a ride each day in Nancy's automobile, which he referred to as a "stink buggy." Once he wrote:

> Friend Mike:
>
> . . . A machine will show folks the man made things but if people want to see Gods own country thave got to get a horse under them. To me the roar of a mountain stream mingled with the bells of a pack trane is grander musick than all the string or brass bands in the world . . .

On the evening of October 24, 1926, they went for a ride in the country. Charlie was holding Jack on his lap. There was a beautiful sunset and he asked Nancy to stop so that he could gaze at it. He watched the sky for a long time, hugging the boy close to him. It was as though he knew that this was the last sunset he would enjoy. Not until the brilliant lights had faded did he ask Nancy to drive on.

Near midnight he complained of pain and Nancy immediately sent for the doctor, but there was nothing anyone could do. In a few minutes it was over.

Charlie had told Trigg that he wanted to be carried

to the cemetery behind horses. A horse-drawn hearse was found in Cascade and a team of black horses was located.

It seemed that the whole land mourned the passing of a beloved friend. Even in the Indian camps the drums beat out a solemn dirge. The shabby, old-fashioned hearse led the procession to the burial grounds. Following it were three saddle horses, two of them ridden by old cowboy friends, Charles Biel and Horace Brewster. The riderless horse carried Charlie's empty saddle with the gun, the lariat, and spurs that were his gear when he rode the range.

Schoolchildren and grownups crowded the sidewalks to watch the long procession. Flags were at half-mast; business houses were closed. The entire town was paying its respects to a beloved and distinguished citizen and friend.

The day had dawned gloomily, with a hint of drizzle in the air, but as the coffin was being lowered the sun suddenly burst through and a beautiful rainbow arched the sky. People murmured at the sight, feeling as if Charlie's spirit were smiling upon them.

So passed a great artist who through his sketches, paintings, and sculpture captured the history of the West during his time.

The Lewistown *Democratic News* on December 16, 1934, printed Will Rogers' tribute to his great friend:

> He wasn't just another artist. He wasn't just another anything. He was a great philosopher. He was a great humorist. He had great underlying spiritual feeling—great sympathy and understanding for the man of the world,

be he Injun or White. He didn't think a paved street made a better town. In people he loved Human Nature. In people he loved Human Interest. He not only left us great living pictures of what our West was, but he left us an example of how to live in friendship with all mankind.

Bibliography

Abbott, E. C., and Smith, Helena Hintington. *We Pointed Them North.* Farrar & Rinehart, New York, 1939.

Adams, Ramon F., and Britzman, Homer E. *Charles M. Russell, the Cowboy Artist.* Trail's End Publishing Co., Pasadena, 1948.

Brummitt, Stella. *Brother Van.* Missionary Education Movement, New York 1919.

Howard, Joseph Kinsey. *Montana Margins.* Yale University Press, New Haven, 1946.

McCracken, Harold, *The Charles M. Russell Book: The Life and Work of the Cowboy Artist.* Doubleday, New York, 1957.

Montana: A State Guide Book. Hastings House, New York, 1939.

Noyes, Al J. *In the Land of the Chinook.* State Pub. Co., Helena, 1917.

Price, Con. *Memories of Old Montana.* Highland Press, Hollywood, 1945.

——.*Trails I Rode.* Trail's End, Pasadena, 1947.

Russell, Austin. *Charles M. Russell, Cowboy Artist, a Biography.* Twayne, New York, 1957.

Russell, Charles Marion. *Rawhide Rawlins Stories.* Montana Newspaper Assn. Great Falls, 1922.

——. *More Rawhides.* Same.

——. *Trails Plowed Under.* Doubleday, Garden City, 1927.

——. *Good Medicine: The Illustrated Letters of Charles M. Russell.* Doubleday, Garden City, 1929.

——. *Pen and Ink Sketches.* Glacier Printing Co., Great Falls, 1945

———. *Pen and Ink Drawings, Books 1 and 2.* Trail's End, Pasadena, 1947.

———. *Rawhide Rawlins Rides Again.* Trail's End, Pasadena, 1948.

Stuart, Granville. *Forty Years on the Frontier.* Edited by Paul C. Phillips. Arthur H. Clark Co., Glendale, 1957.

Yost, Karl. *Charles M. Russell, the Cowboy Artist, a Bibliography.* Trail's End, Pasadena, 1948.

PERIODICALS

Anaconda Standard, December 15, 1901.

Benzein News, November 9, 1917.

Butte Daily Intermountain, Christmas Issue, 1903.

Butte Evening News, Christmas Edition, 1905 (2nd section).

Fergus County Argus (Lewistown) October 18, 1890; February 12, 1891.

Fort Benton River Press, December 22, 1886; January 6 and 12, 1887.

Great Falls Tribune, June 7, 1914; January 15, 1915; October 26, 1926; July 20, 1941; Sunday Supplement ("Montana Parade"), October 14 and 21, 1956.

Hardin Tribune, July 15, 1918.

Harper's Weekly, May 12, 1888.

Helena Weekly Independent, May 5, 1887.

Helena Weekly Herald, May 26, 1887; September 27, 1888.

Helena Record Herald, November 21, 1921.

Lewistown Democratic News, December 16, 1934.

Mineral Argus (of Maiden) July 10, 1884; September 10, 1885.

New York Press, January 31, 1904.

New York Times, April 9, 1911.

St. Louis Missouri Republican, October 5, 1826.

St. Louis Post-Dispatch, December 6, 1903.

Winnet Times, October, 1926.

Index

About the Author

SHANNON GARST was born in Ironwood, Michigan, on July 24, 1899 and moved to Denver, Colorado, at the age of four, where she received most of her schooling. At the age of seventeen she went to Hood River, Oregon, where she taught school for four years. She now lives in Wyoming. Her first acceptances in the field of writing were stories she did for her own children. Since then she has become a versatile writer of juvenile fiction and biography.